PREACHERS ON WHEELS

PREACHER ON WHEELS

Traveling the Road to
Sainthood with Happy Abandon

Paul Hostetler

The Brethren Press, Elgin, Illinois

PREACHER ON WHEELS
Copyright © 1980, by The Brethren Press, Elgin, Ill.
Printed in the United States of America.

Cover Design by Wendell Mathews

Library of Congress Cataloging in Publication Data

Hostetler, Paul, 1925-
  Preacher on wheels.

  1. Hostetler, Eli H. 2. Brethren in Christ—Clergy—
Biography. 3. Clergy—United States—Biography. I. Title.
BX9675.Z8H673   289.9 [B]   79-28086
ISBN 0-87178-716-4

Published by The Brethren Press, Elgin, Illinois 60120

TABLE OF CONTENTS

INTRODUCTION

It seems incongruous that a man's days can be reduced to a few column-inches. Those were my thoughts upon reading the terse facts brought together in my father's obituary. As my mind swept back across the years, I resolved to write a longer (and hopefully more interesting) story of Dad's life. The pages which follow, all too long delayed, are the attempted fulfillment of that promise.

I dislike boring books, especially boring biographies. Fortunately, my writings are never boring. However, my wife and children have been ruthless in putting the ax to some of my most "unboring" tales. And what is even worse, their opinions are almost always sustained by others to whom I go for affirmation. As a result, this book is quite a bit shorter than it once was.

Many of Dad's adventures were so unusual that discerning readers will struggle with a credibility gap. An author of several books who reviewed the manuscript (although assuring me that *he* believed what he had read) expressed concern that others might have difficulty accepting the veracity of certain accounts.

Let me assure you that the story is true, and that any apocryphal details which slipped in because of an overimaginative memory were quickly debunked by my mother (still living) along with my brothers and sisters. Thus the accuracy of the narrative is assured.

I wish to thank my daughter Beth for her valuable assistance in grammar and construction. It is her fortunate ability to dash off lucid prose with little need for revision, while her father manages to mangle the English language in startling fashion at times. I also am grateful to daughter Helen for her typing skills.

Others who have reviewed the manuscript and offered helpful suggestions are Rufus Hollinger and E. Morris Sider. To paraphrase an old saying, "Faithful were the wounds of these friends."

7

And so, bruised ego notwithstanding, I commend these pages to you with the hope that therein you may find inspiration and blessing—and perhaps even a chuckle or two.

Paul Hostetler

Chapter 1

WAGON WHEELS

One of Dad's sermons, typical of his unorthodox ways, had four points rather than the usual three. "This world," he would declare, "has four kinds of people—the rich-rich, the poor-poor, the rich-poor, and the poor-rich."

In each instance the word before the hyphen represented worldly goods and attainment, while the other stood for spiritual values and wealth. Dad always majored on the poor-rich because that was where our family and most others in our small congregation found themselves.

The year was 1935, and I was ten, the eldest of six children. After moving for the ninth time, we were living at the "hilltop place" on the edge of North Lawrence, Ohio. Times were hard, but Dad kept forgetting—like the time he impulsively purchased the four wheels.

A financially astute brother at our church remarked, "Eli Hostetler spends too much money and time on foolish projects." He was right, but he was also wrong. Sometimes people become richer at the same time they become poorer.

The wheels had inflated tires, turned on ball bearings, and were about the size used on heavy wheelbarrows today. Dad cut down an old buggy chassis, mounted the wheels, and put an old wooden door on top.

As can easily be imagined, our wagon went down hills faster than anything in town and was the envy of all children in the community. When families came to our house, the children always begged for rides. We could take the south slope, which was much safer, or the north hill, which was always a daring adventure.

I well remember the day my brother Lloyd had a load of five or six children on the wagon imploring for a trip down the fast hill. The flat top was thirty inches wide and sixty inches long, so there was plenty of room. But it had no rails around the outside.

With all the extra weight, the well oiled wheels picked up speed faster than usual, and the wagon soon began to weave from one side of the gravel road to the other. Nine year old Lloyd didn't upset the wagon, but he was forced to make some frantic turns as each succeeding swerve came closer and closer to the ditches. The screaming children began to tumble off at the rate of one or so each time Lloyd averted a mini-catastrophe.

He did the neatest and fastest job of scattering a half-dozen children I ever saw. It was really funny until the wails of the suffering innocents blended in one strong chorus of protest. Dad comforted the victims and instructed Lloyd to be more careful the next time. He later commented that the happening reminded him of the Bible account where "some fell by the wayside."

The road sloped north from our house for an eighth of a mile and then went up a small grade before dipping off, steeper and much longer. And that hill, like the proverbial mountain, was there waiting to be mastered. When Dad built the wagon he forbade us to coast down that long hill. But as our skills grew, and our importunities increased, he relented.

One sunny afternoon Lloyd, Eli Jr., and I attacked the hill. We rode the wagon down the first slope and coasted to the top of the big one. Then we paused. I was in the driver's seat, but got scared.

Lloyd, who usually had a steadier hand, volunteered to take over, and I quickly agreed. Lloyd sat first, I was second, and Eli had the rear seat. We sat tight against each other, with our legs spread and extending forward past the one in front.

We slo-o-owly eased the eager-to-roll wagon forward. And down the hill we went! The wind was soon whistling past our ears and tears came into our eyes. Before we were half way down the long incline, our four-wheeler was already threatening to break through some kind of barrier. Lloyd was holding her steady as a rock.

Faster and faster we went! Using Dad's metaphor for speed, "The fence posts began flashing by like the stakes of a picket fence!" I looked anxiously down the hill. The bottom was much too far away.

The wagon began to weave ever so little. Then a bit more as Lloyd hung on firmly. I believe we might have made it except for a patch of loose gravel. One big swerve, a desperate effort

10

by Lloyd, and then our charging steed bolted into the right hand ditch.

One moment we were rushing along at many miles per hour. The next moment the front end of the wagon stopped instantly as it thudded into the far bank while the back was flung upward. Lloyd was thrown forward and I went flying over him. Eli almost went into orbit, sailing over both of us!

We slowly picked ourselves up and walked around crying and babbling incoherently. In doctors' terminology, we had many abrasions and contusions but were still ambulatory.

After the initial shock wore off we looked at our pride and joy, our fleet racer. Its front end was badly damaged. The left front wheel wouldn't even turn. Still in a state of confusion, we pulled the wagon out of the ditch and onto the road. We pushed and dragged it slowly back up the two long hills. We cried from the pain of our cuts and bruises, but we ached deep inside for our wounded friend.

Dad was out of the house and saw us coming. He guessed at once what had happened. Sizing up the situation quickly, he noted that we were not seriously hurt. But when he beheld our battered and bleeding parts, noticed our tears and tattered clothes, and examined our vanquished chariot, he cried with us.

Then, when he was sure our hurts would mend, he began to laugh. On, and on. Lloyd, always more good natured, began to laugh too. Then Eli and I joined them. We laughed so long and hard our aches began to feel better.

After things quieted down, Dad's mechanical mind began to size up the damage to the wagon. "I yi yi yi," he said sadly, "that front end is *kaputt*. It will have to be junked. But I have been thinking about a better way to use those wheels anyhow." He had a dreamy look in his eyes, and that meant something good was in the works.

That day he envisioned a miniature car with a front seat and a back seat. With a steering wheel and fenders and bumpers. With headlights and taillights (pretend ones, of course). With a hood and a trunk. And with BRAKES.

A month later his dream was a reality. The little car, about two feet wide and six feet long, was low and sleek. It didn't have a motor, but who cared; we could always push it back up the hill. And cheerfully we did, countless times.

If the wagon made our friends envious, the little car made them positively drool! As I reflect on those days, I marvel that

Dad had the time and money to build the little car. On the other hand, he was just being himself. He understood the delights of his girls and boys because he enjoyed childish pleasures all his days.

We revelled in that little car for a whole year and had plans for many more. But it was not to be.

One day a shiftless farmer brought grain to be ground in Dad's mill. He parked his woebegone car in the sloping driveway. Somehow he forgot to leave his shift lever in low, or reverse, or whatever. As for his emergency brakes, they were in a state of emergency. Our little car was parked under the maple tree nearby.

No one saw it happen. The first warning was a scrunch and then a crash. The old car rolled forward and pushed the little car to the upper bank of the lower driveway. It fell over the three-foot drop and the big car landed right on top of it.

We boys came running. Dad too. Mr. Shiftless, who came walking up slowly, didn't even notice the little vehicle. "It's going to take some doing to get my car out of there," he observed.

Dad was angry. "Don't you have any feelings, Mister? Can't you see what your car has done to the little car under it?" He turned away so old Shiftless wouldn't see his tears.

The little car was smashed and three of the wheels bent beyond repair. Dad later put the surviving one to the sensible use for which it was intended in the first place, mounting it on the front end of a homemade wheelbarrow. Sometimes I would haul my younger brothers and sisters around in it and they would be in high glee. But their bliss was born of ignorance.

On the morning after the accident Dad prayed for his boys at family devotions, asking God to bring us comfort. But then he spoiled the whole thing by praying for Shiftless too.

Chapter 2

MOTORCYCLE WHEELS

Some fathers who do well with their children when they are young, miss it when they become teenagers. They seem to have particular problems with their sons. Here's one way Dad worked at keeping in touch.

George Mohler, a young man at our church, bought a shiny new motorcycle. One day he came to our place and took my two brothers and me for a ride. I decided right then that one day I would get a motorcycle of my own. The summer I turned fifteen I took up the cause in earnest. Dad looked me over with some doubt because my weight with overcoat and boots, and all pockets loaded, was scarcely 120. And besides, money was needed for more essential things.

Lloyd and I kept watching the ads in the paper. One evening we saw a Harley Davidson 74 advertised for $12. Twelve dollars! Dad was sure the price was a misprint, but we convinced him to make the ten-mile trip to the address listed.

Sure enough, the price *was* $12. But the motorcycle was ancient. Dad suggested that it was probably one of the first ones Harley and Davidson put together. It was a huge monster, the very largest and heaviest model. When I sat in the seat, I couldn't touch the ground with both feet.

Furthermore, the motor wasn't in running condition. "That," the smiling advertiser told us, "is because the battery is shot, and so is the generator." He assured us that if we replaced the generator and battery, the old Harley would roar into action. He added that the lights weren't working and that the drive chain sometimes slipped when the rider gunned the machine too much in low gear, but that was mainly caused "by the snortin' power of that 74 engine!"

"Tell you what," he promised, "if you take this Harley home and she won't start, bring 'er back and I'll give your money back." Now that seemed to us boys like a deal which couldn't be beaten.

But Dad still wasn't convinced. "How will we get this thing home if the motor won't run?" he asked. Mr. Friendly Advertiser was equal to the challenge. "Tell you what," he smiled, "I'll lend you a rope to tow 'er home." Dad hesitated. And then Friendly made his final pitch. "And you can keep the rope."

By this time Lloyd and I were in a frenzy. We twisted Dad's arm both literally and figuratively. He finally nodded.

Friendly headed off to his shed for the rope and soon returned with one surprisingly long and thick. Dad tied one end to the car bumper and Friendly tied the other end to the center of the Harley's handlebar.

Dad looked at Lloyd and me, and gave me the nod to get in the saddle since I was a year older and at least five pounds heavier. He clambered into our car and off we went. After driving along in low gear for a while, he shifted into second. When I waved him on, he shifted into high gear and whipped along at thirty miles per hour. The rope held and we arrived home triumphantly.

The next step was to get the motor started. Dad, being Dad, was as eager to crank up the engine as were his boys. Having spent all of twelve dollars, no cash was available to buy either a generator or the special, small-size motorcycle battery. But Dad came through, as always. He pulled the large battery out of our car and hooked it up to the cables on the Harley. I crawled up on the bike, put my foot on the crank, and pushed hard. Nothing. More attempts. Nothing. Dad made some adjustments, and a few kicks later the motor roared into life. It sounded mean, real mean.

We were making progress, but not enough. The motor was running nicely, but the large battery was resting on the driveway beside it. Dad, for obvious reasons, was not willing to have us drag it around by the cables. He found a strong burlap bag, put the battery in it, and tied the top of the bag to the rear fender.

It looked like an abortive attempt at a new brand of saddlebag, but it worked. The big Harley Davidson 74 was finally ready for the road without the indignity of being towed by a car. After we cranked up the motor again, Dad and Lloyd helped get the front end pointed in the right direction.

I climbed aboard, pushed in the clutch, and rammed the hard-to-move shift lever into low gear. Success! The old Harley flew. I went completely around a mile-square country block because of being afraid to turn around on the road. It was pure bliss.

Lloyd, only fourteen years old, conquered the machine next. Then it was Dad's turn. He was much bigger and stronger, and the ride would be a cinch for him, certainly. He got started without incident but couldn't manage to get Harley straightened out. He wobbled from one side of the road to the other, and everywhere between!

After a hundred yards of such disgraceful doings, with us boys laughing until we ached, he stopped and motioned for us to come. A stricken look was on his face. "You can ride this beast if you want to, but not me! I have better things to do." And he meant it; he never rode it again.

We rode the "beast" many more times even though it was much too big and powerful for us. We were always scared of that Harley but wouldn't have admitted it to Dad for anything! One day, long after the generator and battery situation had been corrected, the motor malfunctioned as I was returning home. The trouble seemed to be a fuel stoppage, so I nursed the limping cycle home by closing the choke from time to time.

Just as I was pulling into our driveway, barely chugging along even with the throttle wide open, the fuel suddenly came unstuck. With the staccato of flying gravel stones, the potent engine all at once surged from about half a horse power to a whole herd of stallions!

Inertia pushed me off the seat and onto the back fender while determination and friction kept my hands on the handlebars. I peered ahead from my chest-on-the-seat vantage point and saw our henhouse approaching at a very unsafe speed. Just before the chicken house and Harley came together, I managed to turn enough to avoid hitting the building, but too much to keep control on the loose stones. Bike and henhouse came together in a cloud of dust and noise— and surprisingly little injury!

Not long after that we put up Harley for sale, and a man came to see it the first day. Dad asked him if he would like to drive the thing before he decided on whether to buy it. Potential Buyer agreed.

We got it cranked up and held it steady while he crawled astraddle. What followed next was reminiscent of what happens at the Calgary Stampede when a cowboy rides a bull!

Prospective pushed in the clutch, rammed the gearshift

into low, twisted the throttle on the right handlebar, and he got immediate results. The back wheel was spinning as his bull lunged into motion. Prospective leaned hard to the left as the beast threatened to ram its horns into the high bank across the road.

At the last possible moment, rider and cycle did a beautiful 180 "on a dime with enough room left over to give back a nickel change" as Dad used to say. But this move had his bull charging straight at us, and no clowns were around to distract it. Dad made a remarkable end run (if metaphors may be mixed) in the general vicinity of the mill while we boys scattered in other directions!

When our rider of the purple rage arrived at the spot we had just vacated, he made another 180 and got bucked off. His animal was then lying on its side, giving one long, loud, wide-open roar. Would you believe that Prospective picked himself up, ran over to the Harley, and pulled it upright while it was still in gear with the hammer down? Well he did, and somehow got on top again.

By this time the bull was determined to conclude the matter. It headed straight for our pumphouse. C-R-U-M-P!

The whole thing happened in less than ten seconds. Miraculously, no one was hurt. And we didn't even need to buy an admission ticket for this perfect combination of comedy and bareback riding!

Mr. Prospective Buyer brushed himself off and allowed that he had changed his mind about buying our motorcycle, climbed into his saddle-broken car, and drove slowly into the sunset. He was barely out of earshot until Dad and his sons had one of the best laughs of their years.

We managed to sell that Harley for $25 and used the money for a downpayment on a smaller Harley Davidson. It was light and safe, but not nearly as challenging. Dad wouldn't even ride this tame pony and it was probably for the best. The small motor would have struggled to pull his 200 pounds up the big hills.

Chapter 3

BUGGY WHEELS

According to Maria in *Sound of Music,* the best place to start something is at the beginning. So I'll follow her advice now and pick up this story about my father with one of my earliest memories.

When Dad loaded us all into our family car for the trip to Grandpa Hostetler's farm in Holmes County, Ohio, it was always an adventure. The car was temperamental, the hilly roads unpaved, and the lane an obstacle course.

Although the old home place was only twenty-five miles from our house, childish impatience made it seem much farther away. At long last, however, our lumbering Overland would pass through the eerie shadows of Tramps' Hollow and round the final curve before entering the village of Mount Hope. We would move slowly through the serene atmosphere of the Amish town and then head south for the remaining mile.

The long lane was devoid of gravel stones—just dust or mud—and for some reason most of our excursions came soon after heavy rains. Grandpa got along fine because his horse and buggy were good mudders. But our vehicle was engineered to travel *over* land, not through it.

Dad would get a running start on the narrow road and then swing the car into the lane. The motor roared, the wheels spun, and the mud flew. It was a heart-thumping experience as long as we were in motion. But when the inevitable sudden lurch was followed by the equally inevitable sickening stop, our spirits sank into the slough of despond.

At such moments Dad was the spokesman for us all. Sitting glumly at the wheel, his comment was always "For pity sakes!" That was his favorite form of profanity.

We would slowly crawl out of the car and slog through the mire for the remaining distance. The romance of "to grandfather's house we go" somehow got lost between the bogged-

17

down Overland and the whitewashed picket fence which surrounded the old house.

But our efforts were always well rewarded. Grandma had a bottomless cookie jar, a good supply of toys, and a loving heart. She stood five feet tall, and her circumference was solid evidence of her cooking skills.

After "a good time was had by all" and we were ready to return home, Grandpa would harness his horse and pull our car back on the road. He was much too kind to ever say so, but I am sure he viewed his means of transportation as vastly superior to ours.

My father, Eli H. Hostetler, was born into this Old Order Amish family of eleven children. His parents were poor. Although Dad never said much about it, Henry and Sarah Hostetler must have been very poor indeed. The Amish pride themselves in the farms they own and those they buy for their sons. Grandpa farmed other people's land all his life and never saved enough money to pay toward acreage for his children.

The six girls were known at school as "the poor Hostetler girls," but their patched dresses were always neat and clean. The five boys also wore patched clothes, but their cleanliness was generally ephemeral.

Dad's next older brother was named for his grandfather Solomon who was reputed to be the strongest man in the county. He could pick up two three-bushel bags of wheat, a total of 360 pounds, and carry them up the steps into the feed mill. His namesake, always called Sol, was also strong and one of the best wrestlers in the large Amish community. With little else to be proud of, the Henry Hostetlers bragged about the strength of their two Solomons.

In addition, they perpetuated the legend of a very rich relative in Switzerland who died without any descendants and had provisions in his will for his *fruendshaft* in the New World. A shyster lawyer collected many dollars from various Hostetlers to locate the fortune and was never heard of again.

Another dream of riches was linked to an ancestor of generations past who had a large farm in what is now the heart of Baltimore. The report was that the land was never properly deeded to the city and was thus still owned by the original Baltimore Hostetler's heirs. Of course, nothing ever came of that either.

Dad was born three years before the turn of this century on

18

the twenty-second of January. Somehow the record got mixed up in the old German family Bible, and February was the indicated month. Our family grew up celebrating Dad's and George Washington's birthdays together. The mistake was discovered years later when official proof of birth was needed.

The chopping down the cherry tree legend credited to young George would have suited Dad very well. His mother promised him a much-treasured family heirloom early in life "because Eli always tells the truth." According to his sisters, young Eli showed signs of unusual piety. They pegged this on his determination to defend them from the teasing of their other brothers and his concern for them when they were fearful.

One summer day Katie and Tillie, who were eight and ten, took drinking water to their brother Eli working in a field far from the house. On the way they noticed a huge balloon in the sky. It was slowly descending, and the wind was blowing it toward them. The men in the gondola were hurling sandbags overboard in an attempt to keep the balloon out of the trees. At first the little girls were fearful, then terrified, and finally hysterical as they fled before the threatening monster.

It took a long time for Eli to quiet their fears. The loving concern which he showed his sobbing sisters has remained clearly etched on their souls these many years later. When Aunt Katie related the story to me, she remarked, "You know, Paul, your father was always one to comfort young children when they were hurt or sick."

Somewhere along the line he picked up the nickname "Preach." Not Preacher, just Preach. It seems that a neighbor, Henry Scarr, also a farmer, called him that first. My aunts say it was because Dad was always honest and kind. And because he would go to the woods alone, stand on a stump, and preach to the squirrels and woodpeckers. Furthermore, when they played "church" he was always the preacher.

Uncle Sol, however, has another version of how the nickname got started. He claims that Dad spent so much time daydreaming when hired out to plow for their neighbor that Scarr declared in utter disgust, "You'd better be a preacher since you'll never amount to anything as a farmer!"

I prefer my aunts' account but admit to the possibility of Uncle Sol's revised version.

Dad *was* a dreamer. Even as a boy he was often thinking of

ways to make life better. Sometimes the dreamer and the worker complement each other. At other times they compete. However, the visionary part of God's highest creation is the best. Most anybody can plow a straight furrow, but dreamers travel afar even as they trudge the soil.

The Henry Hostetler family attended church services faithfully. The meetings were held in houses because the Amish have always opposed conducting their services in church buildings. This is based on their historic opposition to ornate cathedrals, often built at the expense of the poor.

The worshippers met in the homes of members with large enough houses. Preparation for the big occasion involved many hours of scrubbing and sweeping, including the house, barn, and sheds. Each farmer did his best to outdo all the rest.

My grandfather's household never had the joy of entertaining the church service. Their house was just too small. At some farms the meetings were held in the barn in warm weather, but Grandfather's barn was little more than an over-size shed.

One characteristic of the Amish service, according to Dad, was the slow pace of the singing. He loved to tell of how a boy could run around the house while one particularly long note was being sung. "Come on, Dad," my brother Lloyd complained, "no song could be that slow!"

Dad was equal to the challenge. "We'll just show you." He and Mother walked out on the porch and instructed Lloyd to get on his mark. They began singing, Mother in her lovely soprano, and Dad in his off-key bass. When they got to the proper note, a long O-o-o-o-o-o-o-o-o-o-o-o-o-h, Lloyd took off around the house.

Mother and Dad hung on until Lloyd came dashing back across his starting point. Their faces were looking a bit strained, and their volume was somewhat diminished, but they had proven their point beyond any reasonable doubt.

When getting ready for the church service, the Amish hosts set up rows of crude benches without backrests. Since the meetings were three hours in duration because of the slow singing and lengthy sermons delivered by two or more preachers, backs began to ache long before the closing prayer.

Some worshippers would fall asleep, at times leaning on the one beside them. One old codger simply leaned his head

20

against the back of the one sitting in front of him.

One Sunday the young men conspired against this sleeper. They came into the house and sat on the bench ahead of him, arranging their seating so that one was sitting directly in front, with some space beside. The service moved along, and in due time the 20th Century Eutychus parked his head against the willing back of the conspirator.

The young women were also in on the scheme and were hardput to suppress their giggles. After a good long wait to ensure Sleeper's total relaxation, the young man supporting the sagging head suddenly moved forward and slid sideways. Sleeper's head hit the bench with a resounding thump! A woman jumped, a child started to cry, and the young people snickered, moaning for full release to their mirth.

Sleeper struggled to his feet, all the while rubbing the reddening spot on his forehead. The preacher, surmising that he was being challenged for the floor, stopped in mid-sentence. But Sleeper wasn't interested in preaching—his own or anyone else's. All he wanted was a fast way outdoors. Still half asleep, he staggered to the nearest exit. The preacher resumed his sermon, but he might as well have called it a day.

Of all the Amish services Dad attended in his youth, this was the only one he ever mentioned.

Chapter 4

AUTOMOBILE WHEELS

Dad's interests turned to courtship and automobiles almost simultaneously. In the eyes of his parents and friends the former was not only natural, but good. The latter, however, was worldly and not allowed among the Amish. But he bought one notwithstanding.

His parents were vexed by this departure from the traditions of the elders, but they suffered mostly in silence. Not so with Uncle Eli (for whom Dad had been named) on the adjoining farm. Uncle Eli Hostetler's buildings were about an eighth mile from the road. Dad's old home place was about a quarter mile from the same road.

To save the expense of building two long lanes, the two farms had a joint lane which came past Uncle Eli's place and then extended on to the other homestead. Well, when Dad and some of his brothers began to raise dust and make loud car-noises in their comings and goings, Uncle Eli came over to my grandfather's house and spoke some stern words to his brother.

"You either stop your boys from driving their ungodly automobiles past my house or else build yourself a new lane." Grandpa Hostetler, like Isaac of old, wanted peace so he made a new lane—a full quarter-mile long. He discreetly placed it at the line fence farthest from his irate brother. Henceforth when his errant sons used their cars, Uncle Eli was spared the dust and noise—and maybe even an ulcer!

One night Dad used his new car to court a girl. He proudly wheeled into the lane of the farm where she lived and promptly ran over a small heifer, stopping the vehicle just after the front wheels passed over it. The girl's father came running out of the house and helped get the offensive car off the bawling calf which amazingly was not hurt very much. That was the last time Dad dated that farmer's daughter.

He dated other girls of his home church, but none seemed

to be the one for him. Then one day when he was with a group of Conservative Amish Mennonite young people in a neighboring community, he spied a beautiful lass who captured his fancy from the very first.

Most people would see little difference between the Amish of Holmes County and the Conservative Amish Mennonites of Stark County, but the two groups felt their differences very keenly. For a young man of one fellowship to marry a young woman of the other was *Verboten*. A real no-no.

In Mother's own words, "Nevertheless, we dated each other with the blind faith of youth that all things would work out some time in the future. But soon a dark cloud blotted out the bright sun of our happy anticipations. Because of a few minor disagreements and differences between our churches, my parents told me that our courtship must end. Yet, with the determination of youth we exchanged letters with each other until that was also forbidden."

As you can see, Mother placed the blame on religious differences. I think there was an additional problem. My mother's parents, George and Lena Yoder, were much better "fixed" financially, and they had two children. Dad's parents had a scarcity of most everything except children—eleven of them. Even among the Amish, who hold that matches for matrimony are made in heaven, the people of means generally marry each other, and the poor take what is left.

Dad and Mother eloped. The Hostetlers were surprised and bemused. The Yoders were distressed and angry. The fact remained, however, that their offspring had run off to New Albany, Indiana, and found an obliging person with authority to legalize the marriage despite two pairs of perturbed parents.

Again in Mother's words, "We returned to Ohio as Mr. and Mrs. E. H. Hostetler to the chagrin of our parents. We furnished a small house with a few pieces of furniture, but to us it was home. Even though we later realized that it was wrong to go against the wishes of our parents, at the time it seemed right. My husband and I have both asked for forgiveness which has very graciously been given to us. We thank the Lord that all concerned are now happy." (This was written in 1948.)

During the first few months of their marriage, Dad and Mother lived near Hartville, and Dad worked in a stone quarry. One day he was prying rocks loose which had been blasted but had not fallen to the level below. As he was busy at his task he suddenly noticed a huge rock directly above his head begin to move. He desperately looked for a quick way out. There was none! He watched the rock with pounding heart. It stopped! Dad crawled out of the dangerous spot as quickly as possible.

Then the boulder, which must have weighed tons, came crashing down.

As he stood nearby in safety, he trembled with terrible fear. "My knees shook until they buckled under me," Dad would say, "just like Belshazzar in the Bible when he saw the handwriting on the wall." Dad had a rousing sermon on Belshazzar in later years in which he always included his stone quarry experience.

He sat down on the rocks until his knees lost their rubber and promised God that he would become more obedient. But, as generally happens in such scare situations, his promise was not carried out.

Sometime later Dad and Mother, along with two other people, were on a trip late at night. Dad was driving with everyone else asleep. He came to a railroad crossing and stopped because there were no signals. When he put the car in low gear to cross the tracks, the motor stopped. Wondering what could have caused it, he stepped on the starter. But, for some reason the starter wouldn't work either.

Annoyed, he got out of the car with crank in hand. Just as he reached the front of the car a fast passenger train came rushing past within a few feet of where he stood! He jumped back into the car to get away from the noise and the soot. After the train passed by, Dad tried the starter again. It worked, and the car started. He was soon on his way—with all the others still asleep.

When Dad related this story, he would pause dramatically. "God stopped that motor. God held back that starter. God saved our lives!"

All his life Dad was on wheels. To change the metaphor, for him the grass was always greener on the other side of the fence. He and Mother lived in a dozen and a half different places, and he got involved in as many different jobs.

A few months after they were married, my Grandfather Yoder convinced Dad and Mother to move into his farmhouse near Greentown and work on the farm. Dad farmed and helped fix up many things around the place, but his heart wasn't really in it. My oldest sister, Mary Ellen, was born there in the second year of their marriage. When she was still a tiny tot, she could sing unusually well, just like her mother and Grandmother Yoder.

Soon after Mary Ellen's birth, Dad's feet got itchy again. He and Mother decided to build a house. Mother says rather wistfully that this little house was "beautiful inside and out. All the wood was light and shiny, and there was plenty of cupboard space."

In spite of all that, Dad again hankered for a new location. The reason given was to get nearer Hartville where close friends and relatives lived. So they purchased a lot and "built everything up from scratch again." They were living there in 1925 when I was born. Second child—fourth house. Dad ventured into the chicken business. He and Mother built several round brooder houses and raised broilers.

In 1926 Mother was pregnant again, and Dad was looking to other fields. He and my Uncle Joe Mast decided to move to Alden, New York (near Buffalo), build a large chicken house for laying hens, and start producing White Leghorn eggs in a big way.

My Aunt Amanda says the real reason Uncle Joe wanted to move to New York was so that he could have a car. Mother's comment on this venture was a sigh of resignation: "So off we went."

Dad and Mother bought a place near Alden and began attending the nearby Conservative Mennonite Church. Our family and Uncle Joe's family lived in the same large house. Dad and Uncle Joe built their huge henhouse, filled it with hens, and were on their way to bigger and better things. But the hens got sick, real sick. Many died, and the rest quit laying. And that was the end of Dad's career as a big time egg producer.

My earliest memory comes out of those difficult days. Because of the financial reverses with the chickens, the bank needed to bring pressure for repayment of borrowed funds. One day Dad and Mother made a trip to the bank to ask for more time on an overdue note. They took me along, thinking I was too young to understand what was happening.

I remember the banker as being stern and unyielding when my parents pleaded for more time to make the demanded payment. Dad did everything but get down on his knees before that bank official, but he would not relent. As we left his well appointed office, I had the dreadful feeling that all of us were headed for fiscal catastrophe. Those fears lingered through the years.

The Alden, New York move would need to be written off as a total disaster except for one saving feature. Depressed though they were financially, Dad and Mother struck gold spiritually.

An evangelistic meeting was being conducted in a large tent pitched in Clarence Center, about twenty-five miles away. Sponsored by the Brethren in Christ Church of the small village, the evangelist was the Reverend Ray I. Witter from Kansas. With a deep longing for better things in his spiritual life, Dad took Mother to the meetings.

Mother's attendance was interrupted at the end of the first week when Lloyd was born in July of 1926. In that day mothers were kept in bed much too long after childbirth. Mother, however, was determined to get back to the inspiration of the tent meetings. She missed the second week, but attended the third and final week, carrying week-old Lloyd with her. No wonder he ended up being a preacher!

Dad and Mother found the Lord in a new way during those meetings, but they were still stopping short of a complete consecration of their lives to God. As Mother records it, "We had not gone the whole way with God and straightened our past life. Then God took matters in His own hands and brought conditions to a crisis. Eli was stricken with diptheria and became so ill he thought his days were numbered.

"He called to God for help and God pointed out some sins which must be confessed and some restitutions which had to be made. He promised God to make a clean sweep and he meant it.

"God honored that prayer and promise, and healed him of his diptheria. In his ignorance he told friends later that 'even though the Bible doesn't say anything about making restitution, it sure made me feel good!' Upon arising from his sick bed, my husband took the neglected Bible off the shelf and instituted our family altar. It has never ceased to this day."

Not long after that Mother also made a total commitment to the Lord. I often heard them tell of how thrilled they were with their new experience. They boldly ventured forth with great confidence in a great God. When they needed something which they felt was God's will, they fasted and prayed until the answer came.

They claimed God as their healer, and their faith was honored with truly miraculous healings. I many times heard Dad relate in public meetings how I tumbled out of the family car one day while it was parked near the house, and broke my arm. Dad set the bone and tied a splint on it as I screamed in pain.

After I was put to bed, still yelling loudly, Dad and Mother knelt nearby and prayed for the healing of that arm. I suddenly quieted down and went to sleep. The next day they put my arm in a sling and let me go outside to play. "The next thing we knew," Dad would testify with tears streaming down his face, "here comes little Paul around the corner of the house dragging a large branch with his broken arm—now completely healed!"

In their boldness as new Christians they made rash statements about never needing a doctor or hospital again. Their declarations brought severe criticism from friends, and turbulent testings later on.

Our family struggled on into 1927. Eli Jr. was born in November. Dad was working at odd jobs here and there. Somehow Ohio looked greener from the New York side of the fence, especially when Grandpa Yoder beckoned. He was, in fact, sending out desperate signals for help to harvest a large celery crop. Dad felt like rolling again so the family of six moved back to Ohio.

In the fall of 1928 Mary Ellen became ill with a serious mastoid infection. Friends urged Mother and Dad to take her to a doctor, but they held firmly to their convictions. They fasted and prayed. They just knew that God would again come through for them as He had in the past.

But He didn't.

Mary Ellen died.

Although only three years old, I remember this sad happening vividly. I recall the sound of weeping in another room. After a while Dad and Mother came out of the room. They were haggard. They were defeated. Dad took me by the hand and led me into the room where they wept as I wondered.

It was just as though someone had turned off the lights in their hearts. Their little singer had slipped away. No longer would they be able to have Mary Ellen sing her clear childish soprano while Mother sang alto and Dad bass. But the profound shock of God disappointing their fervent faith was even more distressing.

My next memory is the funeral. Mary Ellen was in a box which was placed across the end of two front pews as the people walked past. Dad carried me to the box, and I looked at my sister for the last time. It was sad, but I remember being more concerned for my parents than feeling upset with the loss. We wended our way to the cemetery beside the church. The box was lowered into a hole twelve feet deep as measured with the yardstick of a three-year old.

Why did God allow this tragedy to come into our home? I never asked my parents, but here are my conclusions. God is pleased with devoted, radical Christians. He needs more of them. Mother and Dad were devoted, radical Christians, but they were moving dangerously close to the precipice of fanaticism. They almost fell over.

Then God mercifully reached out and took Mary Ellen home, striking dismay and sorrow deep into their hearts. But the bane was a blessing. Dad and Mother, though in a state of shock for many days, finally recovered with an even stronger faith. Once again their favorite song was Fanny Crosby's "Blessed assurance, Jesus is mine! O what a foretaste of Glory divine!" Now, however, they sang it with more meaning to both themselves and others.

Not long ago Mother and I stood at Mary Ellen's grave. The small stone is badly weathered. It says simply: "Dear Mary Ellen Hostetler, 1923-1928." Mother told me again of how beautifully Mary Ellen used to sing. "The louder your dad and I sang," she said with trembling lips, "the louder Mary Ellen sang!"

I wondered, "Mother, do you think she is a child in heaven now, or a grown woman more than fifty years old?" Mother was startled. It was a new thought. "I can think of her only as a child," she mused.

As we moved slowly away, I thought of a few lines which would be a suitable epitaph for Little Sister, caught away after only five short summers, and which must have an answering echo in the hearts of other parents who have laid away their little ones.

Soft breezes, blow gently,
Take care, take care,
For fond, fond hopes
Lie buried there.

Less than a year after Mary Ellen died, Mother gave birth to her fifth child. How pleased she and Dad were that God gave them another little girl in exchange for the one He had called to Himself. They named her Lois Fern, and although she never sang as Mary Ellen had in her early years, she soon gave evidence of also having a lovely voice.

Chapter 5

TRACTOR WHEELS

Dad's youngest sister, Lydia, was fifteen years old in 1928. One day she met Willie J. Myers, pastor of the Sippo Brethren in Christ Church, located between Massillon and North Lawrence, Ohio. Pastor Myers made a very forceful impression on the teenager as "a man of God." She told Pastor Myers about her older brother, Eli, and suggested that he talk with him.

A revival meeting was in progress at the Sippo Church with Abner Martin of Elizabethtown, Pennsylvania serving as the evangelist. Only a handful of people were attending because the congregation had suffered a serious set-back not long before when Russelism (now Jehovah's Witnesses) ensnared most of the members, including the pastor's wife.

Grandfather Yoder and Dad were working in the celery fields when they noticed two men coming toward them dressed in Sunday clothes. Dad kept working, assuming that they had come to see Grandpa Yoder. However, they were looking for Eli Hostetler.

Willie Myers introduced himself and the evangelist. When Abner Martin shook Dad's hand he said, "Praise the Lord, Brother Eli!" Dad, a bit surprised at so direct a greeting from a stranger, liked the approach very much and quickly replied in a similar vein.

That evening marked our family's first trip to the small Sippo Church at the corner of State Route 93 and Cherry Road (today called Wooster Avenue). It was the first in a long series of revival meetings Dad and Mother attended in various churches whenever they were within driving distance during our growing-up years. I have many recollections of either sitting or lying on hard church pews while Dad was calling out his enthusiastic "That's the truth, brother" to the preacher and then helping people "pray through" who responded to the invitation at the end of the sermon.

Well, before the Sippo meeting was over, Dad and Mother, Jonas and Lizzie Hostetler, John and Katie Helmuth, Joe and Anna Slabaugh, and Lydia Hostetler were all attending. When Lizzie first saw Abner Martin with his beautiful full beard, she exclaimed, "This church is no good; they have an Amish preacher!" She soon learned that although Brother Martin looked like an Amish preacher, his sermons were just what she was hoping for.

The group were scattered more than forty miles from each other, but they began to get together regularly for prayer meetings. This came about partly because they were being shunned in their home churches. The meetings were lively and long. John Helmuth was leading the meeting one night when everyone present had led in prayer. When they rose from their knees, he looked at the clock and said, "It's not yet midnight, so let's sing some more songs."

According to John, Dad even then showed clear signs of pastoral leadership and preaching ability. While his remarks in no way agreed with his Wesleyan theology, John declared, "Eli Hostetler was predestined to preach."

The pastors of their home churches did not look on the prayer meeting activity with approval. In fact, they brought about "cease and desist" pressures which finally resulted in all of the prayer meeting families leaving their churches permanently.

The welcome mat was out at the Sippo Church, but it was far from where the families lived. This gave Dad a ready reason for moving again. He found a 42-acre farm with ten acres of rich black soil (muck farm) a few miles north of North Lawrence and about seven miles from the Sippo Church. Not long after we moved to the farm, Uncle Jonas and Dad built another house for their family. Joe Slabaughs also moved into the vicinity of the Sippo Church. John Helmuths did not move nearer then, but they and all the other families soon joined the Sippo Brethren in Christ Church.

One day I heard a neighbor use an interesting combination of words. I rolled them over in my mind and waited for an opportune time to use them. That opportunity came at the noon meal. Dad prayed the blessing on the food, and in the brief silence which followed his Amen I carefully said, "Son - of - a - bitch."

The stunned look on Dad's face caused me to suspect that my four words were something less than acceptable. My tentative conclusion was all too correct. Dad grabbed me and marched me to another room for the administration of the Biblical rod technique. I returned to the table firmly impressed with the necessity of clean speech—especially after prayers.

Dad and Uncle Jonas did truck farming together, taking the produce to a farmers market in Massillon. True to pattern, Dad dropped out of that business a few years later, but Jonas continued in the market business all his life, eventually building a store across the road from the church.

Dad built the first of his many "inventions" on the muck farm. He rigged up a tractor by motorizing a horse-drawn corn cultivator. It was an awkward, strung out affair which worked very well while cultivating long rows, but couldn't turn around easily at the end of the field.

As a pre-school boy, I was proud of the invention, but was terribly deflated the day Uncle Jonas disgustedly declared that "the thing takes a ten acre field to turn around in."

The tractor was also hard to get out of gear once it was going. Because of this it demolished a number of line fences and once ended up in the small creek bordering the farm. One day the contrivance almost finished Dad off. He was backing it into the upper part of the barn, and when he tried to disengage the reverse gear, it stuck.

The tractor moved slowly toward the open door at the other side of the barn floor as Dad struggled with the clutch and shift lever. Suddenly the seat, which extended behind the rear wheels, was projecting out through the opening over a full-story drop to the stone barnyard below! The iron cleats of the power wheels began chewing at the small plank which anchored the bottom of the doorway.

The wheels would almost climb over, and then slip back again. As Dad struggled desperately with his bucking bronc, he knew that if the wheel cleats took hold, the tractor would go through the opening and crush him on the hard surface below.

He prayed a panic prayer similar to sinking Peter's, and God told him—for goodness sake—to turn off the ignition key! Dad lunged and twisted the key just as the cleats were finally getting a better grip. The engine died and Dad lived. For many moments he sat on the seat suspended over space and thanked God for sparing his life.

The tractor was put out to pasture. Uncle Jonas had refused to drive it before the barn incident, and Dad was in full agreement after. As I recall, the invention oxidized in peace for quite a long time until a junk man offered a few dollars for it. No doubt, the steel in the cantankerous contraption was reincarnated in a more successful form.

Uncle Jonas and Dad later bought an old Fordson tractor, a heavy, hard to steer monster. This point was dramatically demonstrated when the back wheels promptly broke through the farm bridge which crossed the deep ditch draining the muck land. Fortunately Uncle Jonas, who was in the driver's seat, was not injured.

The problem of how to get the mechanical ox out of the four-foot ditch was difficult indeed. Dad scratched his head a while and came up with a plan. He marshalled the forces of our car, Uncle Jonas' car, the small farm truck, and the car of a neighbor. The truck was hooked to the embarrassed tractor, then a car to the front bumper of the truck, and so on.

Uncle Jonas carefully climbed on the old Fordson which had its radiator aimed in the general direction of the midday sun. Dad, standing in full view of all the drivers, gave the signal. Wheels spun and the black dirt flew! The Fordson grudgingly moved about a foot and slowly settled back into place.

Dad scratched his head some more and decided that additional traction was needed. So the call went out for all the women and children to get into the back seats of the cars. We did this in high excitement. Even a few dogs jumped in.

When the second signal was given, the result was much better until the chain at the tractor snapped. The truck and three cars surged forward and all of us yelled in victory. The Fordson thunked back into the ditch. "For pity sakes!" complained Dad.

Every vehicle was slowly backed into place and a heavier chain secured to tractor and truck. The third signal was given, and this time the Fordson was jerked out of its disgrace. "Isn't that the berries!" Dad exclaimed, as he often did when nothing else could express his feelings as well.

The Fordson episode was the most exciting event that ever happened on the muck farm except for a brief attempt at founding a nudist colony.

One warm day my two younger brothers and I and our three male cousins had a conference behind the outhouse. Someone made the intriguing suggestion that we take off all our clothes and run to the barn. The motion was seconded and the vote unanimous.

We crowded into the privy (a somewhat limited two-seater) and disrobed. Then, with the eldest—aged six—in the lead, we dashed single file across the lawn and down the driveway to the barn! Three year old Eli Jr., Dad's namesake, brought up the rear, trailing far behind.

All was well except that Mother happened to be looking out the window. She came charging out to the barn and her feelings were not favorable. After she finished laying her hands on our bare bottoms, our feelings were not favorable either!

"Where are your clothes?" she asked as she considered our sinful state. "Out there, inside the toilet," volunteered Cousin Jack. "Should we go back and put them on?"

Mother was aghast. Allow her sons to make another spectacle of themselves? Never. (The nearest neighbor was beyond the next hill and completely out of sight.) "You just wait right here until I bring your clothes to you."

When Dad came in from the fields at noon, Mother described our indecent exposure in full detail. She suggested that he give us another licking, but he declined, mostly because he was laughing too much. After a bit Mother laughed too, and then it was safe for us to join in.

Chapter 6

TOY WHEELS

My mind skips lightly back across the decades to the excitement of Christmas time. Candy and nuts come to remembrance first. These were always scarce at our house because money was carefully saved for more sensible food. At Christmas, however, all laws of finance and health were cheerfully broken. Candy was sitting around, just begging to be devoured.

And bananas. And oranges. These delicious fruits were usually divided out at other times, say a one-third banana per person, with Mother going without so that our pieces could be bigger. No wonder she barely tipped a hundred pounds.

Christmas time brought whole bananas and whole oranges, and the opportunity to go back for more. Combined with the candy and nuts, the result was always a delightful stomach ache. When that ache was topped off with the Christmas dinner, the discomfort was pure boyish bottomless-pit-appetite bliss!

Ah, the ecstasy and the agony!

In the late 20's and early 30's the gifts were few, but the quality of the anticipation and fulfillment was high indeed. The first Christmas I remember was my fourth one. Each of us children got much needed clothing, and I got a red toy truck with yellow wheels that turned.

But the new clothes, and even the truck, were laid aside when Dad brought out a final surprise package. Eager hands tore off the wrappings and opened the box. And wonder of wonders—a little toy accordian lay nestled in the tissue paper!

The Christmas concert began at once and lasted for days, threatening the mental health of Mother and Dad. I learned to play "Silent Night," and Dad stretched the truth by declaring it sounded like the real thing. Before long the little red accordian broke. It was a sad day for its accomplished players. For some strange reason Dad, who could and would repair almost anything, just never got around to working on the instrument.

Christmas at our church always involved two activities which brought great excitement to children and adults. One was the treat handed out to all at the end of the last Sunday morning service before Christmas. It was the longest meeting of the year! The antique clock on the wall tick-tocked the minutes away with tortoise-like slowness.

The great moment would finally come. The deacons and their helpers struggled in with boxes bulging with the prized bags. Each bag had an orange, a popcorn ball, and pieces of candy in quality, quantity, and variety enough to delight even the most Scrooge-like adult.

After all had received their share of the loot, Deacon Jonas would always clear his throat and announce, "If any members of your family are missing, please come and get bags for them."

That was fine with me with one exception. A family who lived about half-way between our church and the Mennonite Church two miles away, usually attended our Sunday School. But about a month before Christmas each year they would deploy half their forces to the Mennonite Church.

On Christmas Sunday half of the family would attend each church—and collect treats for the ones at the other church. I was very indignant about this, and some adults were unhappy also. The deacons and ministers, however, and other large-hearted souls simply smiled and cheerfully gave the Christmas treats to the connivers.

Since Sunday evening services at the Sippo Church were on alternate Sunday nights, our family often attended the Mennonite Church on the off-nights. Unfortunately, Dad didn't respond to the suggestion that this qualified us for double treats too!

When we arrived home from church with our treats, Mother would get a large, colorful dish out of the cupboard, and then all family members emptied the total contents of the bags into the dish. The result was overpoweringly mouth-watering as the candy spilled over the edges. Dad's rule was that the candy was for all as long as it lasted, and its existence on earth was remarkably short.

One year we persuaded Dad to let each person keep his

own bag. He agreed, reluctantly. Some of our bags were empty long before others. Neither those who emptied their bags first nor those who ate more slowly had much fun. Always afterward the deep and wide dish was hauled out and loaded with candy. That Christmas tradition, so typical of Dad's own philosophy, holds salivation capabilities even now.

The second activity which brought excitement to our church at Christmas was the program. Each child and teenager had a part in this evening service. The children usually had recitations in groups, often holding a letter or picture which somehow managed to be upside down or backwards, or both, to the great delight of all except the confused children's parents.

The children in the different age groups often sang a familiar carol. This worked well because of the safety of numbers. However, one year when I was about four, my Aunt Lydia decided to match me up with a cute little girl, Ruthie Kohr, for a duet. Although I was rather cool to the idea, I went along at the rehearsal stage.

The night of the program was another matter. They stood the two of us on the platform together and then cued us for "Away in a Manger." Ruthie wouldn't sing without me, and I wouldn't sing. Aunt Lydia was persistent, but I was adamant.

Then Dad decided to help. He got my attention from where he was sitting near the front of the church. He first offered me a nickel if I would sing. Even though that brought visions of five lollipops, I shook my head. Some people who heard Dad's stage whisper, laughed. Dad upped his ante to a dime, but I again shook my head.

In desperation he increased the bribe to a quarter, an astronomical amount of cash. It was in vain. By that time I was beyond the point of being enticed by filthy lucre of any amount. I was finally released, burning with shame, and Aunt Lydia's star attraction for the evening went aglimmering.

When we got home from church, Dad took me off to the side and told me how sorry he was for what had happened. He then reached into his pocket and gave me a penny "to help you feel better." It worked, and my recovery was complete. The next Christmas I sang "Away in a Manger"—with fifteen others.

Christmas at our house always happened on Christmas

morning. Dad and Mother would have nothing to do with Santa Claus or Christmas trees, dismissing them as pagan. Some friends felt that we children were deprived of important Christmas customs, but our happiness was undimmed by the lack of the jolly red man and his reindeer. We also got along very well without a tree.

The emphasis was on Christ coming to earth as a baby in a manger. The reading of the Christmas story from St. Luke and St. Matthew was a regular part of Christmas day activities. The prayer which followed went a long way toward keeping the holy holiday in proper perspective. Christmas was a time for permitted stomach aches, but it was also a time for directed learning in things which really mattered.

Chapter 7

TRUCK WHEELS

Soon after joining the Sippo Brethren in Christ Church, Dad was urged to attend the annual General Conference and get acquainted with the brotherhood. He resolved to go. In June of 1929 he travelled to his first General Conference, held in Merrill, Michigan, and in a barn at that.

He represented the Sippo Church as the official delegate, but his highest pleasure came from attending the nightly evangelistic meetings conducted in a large tent. The preacher sounded forth the Word, and Dad could be counted on to support him all the way with his exuberant Amens.

Pastor Willie Myers and Uncle Jonas were also present from the Sippo Church. One night an enthusiastic but uniformed brother arranged for the three men to sing in the tent meeting. Pastor Myers sang a beautiful tenor, Jonas a so-so melody, and Dad a wishful bass. They sang "Jonah and the Whale" and somehow managed to get Jonah on dry land!

Before they sang, Dad told one of his favorite stories:

A little girl was singing "Jonah and the Whale" with obvious delight, especially the part which goes, "And he'll tell us all about it over there." A skeptic asked her how she knew the story was true. "Because it's in the Bible," she promptly replied, "and when I get to heaven I'm going to sit down beside Jonah and ask him all about his ride inside the whale!"

The skeptic frowned. "But what if Jonah isn't in heaven when you get there?" Quick as anything the little miss responded. "Then *you* ask him!"

The next June the General Conference convened at the Air Hill Church near Chambersburg, Pennsylvania. By that time Dad had purchased a new Model-A truck with a stake bed. Still tingling with the joys of the Michigan conclave, Dad convinced a group to travel to this conference on the back part of his truck enclosed with a canvas canopy.

He had his first encounter with the narrow roads and steep hills of the Pennsylvania mountains on that pilgrimage. As the truck was grinding its way up the long slope of the first mountain, the radiator overheated and boiled over. Dad was pleased to notice a lad with a pail of water nearby. After refilling the radiator, Dad thanked the boy and decided to give him a penny. "That'll be five cents," said the young businessman with outstretched hand.

A nickel was a lot of money in those days, and Dad was sorely tried. In the next valley he purchased a five-gallon can for such contingencies and never needed to buy water again.

The truck slowly clambered up the next mountain, stopping for a fill-up of water, and I-thought-I-coulded down the other side. As they were whipping along, Mother, who was riding under the canvas at the time, lost her bonnet out the back of the truck. She screamed, and everyone joined in the clamor to get the truck stopped.

Dad was sure someone had fallen overboard, so he jammed on the brakes hard. The hill was steep, and the wheels were smoking when they finally screeched to a stop. After the truck was turned around, they slowly low-geared it all the way back to the fallen bonnet which someone had obligingly run over before knocking it off the road.

Dad looked at it ruefully and said sadly in good Pennsylvania Dutch, "I yi yi yi yi." Bonnets were hard to come by, so Mother carefully remolded it as they travelled on. They slowly completed the 350-mile trip to the Air Hill Church. Dad was again the Sippo delegate and again revelled in the evangelistic meetings.

Someone at that General Conference impressed him with the importance of going into the highways and byways to compel people to attend church. After returning home, the truck became a people-mover on Sunday mornings and evenings. This was exciting for us children in warm weather, but as the fall coolness turned into the chills of winter, our enthusiasm congealed.

Northern Ohio temperatures dip below zero Fahrenheit in January and February, and many times we passengers sitting on the hay covered floor of the truck got very cold. To keep from freezing altogether, we sang gospel songs and choruses. " 'Tis the Old Time Religion" was a favorite because we could make up verses as we went along. A typical verse was:

It was good for our fathers,
It was good for our fathers,
It was good for our fathers,
And it's good enough for me!

Everyone would then join in the chorus, " 'Tis the old time religion (three times), And it's good enough for me!"

We would continue: It was good for our mothers, brothers, sisters, cousins, uncles, aunts, *ad infinitum*. Other verses were: "It will take us home to heaven, Makes me love everybody, It will do when I am dying." My favorite was, "It was good for *Paul* and Silas."

I learned to sing vibrato at a very tender age with the assistance of teeth chattering in the cold!

What a sight and sound we must have made as we drove through the streets of North Lawrence, collecting people who were motivated enough to ride to church in a cold truck. I can remember feeling a bit uneasy about the whole thing, but being proud of Dad and the new truck. It became a lifetime practice for him. Even after he no longer had the truck, he would jam extra passengers into our car or make additional trips.

My first memories of the family altar come from the muck farm setting. Each morning before breakfast Dad would get out the Bible and read the lesson suggested as the daily reading in the Sunday School quarterly. Then we all knelt and he or Mother prayed out loud. They prayed for many concerns, and their prayers were long enough to make for swollen knees, but they never neglected to pray for their children, mentioning each one by name.

The Biblical (and German) tradition of strict obedience to parents was one of the virtues emphasized at the family altar. Dad would illustrate this command with the story of the prophet in the Bible who disobeyed God and was promptly killed by a lion. Or the children who showed disrespect to Prophet Elisha and were mauled by bears.

Today's teachers frown on such child psychology, asserting it will bring needless fears into children's minds. They may be right. I remember having dreams which included lions and bears, but the importance of obedience has always been with me.

Other, harder lessons involving first-hand experience also helped. One day brothers and cousins were playing in the barn. We began to fool around with the three-pronged pitch fork despite warnings from Dad to keep our hands off. When we finished playing with the forbidden tool, we set it against the haymow with the prongs up.

We then climbed up into the mow which was only six feet high with hay. After we tired of playing on the hay someone called out, "The last one out is a rotten egg!" Never willing to be a rotten egg, I went tearing across the mow, barely ahead of the others, and slid over the edge for the jump to the barn-floor. The carelessly placed fork awaited me.

A prong rammed deep into my thigh as I tumbled to the floor. One of the boys grabbed the handle and yanked it out, and then we ran for the house. But things began to spin and, the next thing I knew, Mother was sitting on the lawn beside me, very much concerned. No scolding. No moralizing. Only loving care. She realized I "had learned my lesson."

Later that same summer we boys were crawling up the ladder at the side of the mow and jumping down on the soft hay from the high beams above. Only we older boys were allowed to jump. My brother, Lloyd, begged to be allowed also. I finally relented, notwithstanding parental prohibitions.

After several successful jumps, Lloyd and I crawled back up on the beam again. Lloyd said, "Look Paul, I am going to jump as far as you did last time!" He inched his foot back on the ten-inch beam to get more leverage for the jump. In his eagerness he moved it back just a bit too far. With a flailing of arms he tumbled off. Like in a slow-motion movie, Lloyd did a somersault and thudded to the floor twelve feet below. He lay there motionless except for some twitching, and one arm had an elbow where it was usually straight.

Mother and Dad were soon on the scene. They carefully lifted Lloyd and carried him to the house. After a while he regained consciousness. Fortunately, his concussion symptoms cleared away in a few days, but the splint on his broken arm remained a constant reminder of the follies of disobedience.

Dad often said, "Boys will be boys!" and he was probably right. While living on the muck farm, we boys were told to never, never attempt to operate the motorized equipment. However, when Cousin Ervan was nine years old, he was allowed to drive the small farm truck when his dad was with him.

One day when all adults were gone to the city, we younger

cousins and brothers begged Ervan to drive the truck. He resisted for a long time but eventually gave in to the pressures of hero-worship. After he drove the truck around slowly for a while, someone got the notion to put sticks under the back wheels while the truck was in motion.

Ervan's little brother Paul was enjoying the fun as a four year old. All was well until Ervan drove the truck up the barn-hill. Since the truck had a part-load of gravel, the pull was harder than he anticipated. The motor choked down, and the truck began to roll backwards. We all scampered away except little Paul. The back wheel knocked him down and rolled over him—right over his head.

Little Paul was carried to their house and a neighbor called. I shall never forget the sight of the blood trickling out of his ear. The neighbor called a doctor, and he was there when our parents came home. When suppertime came, Ervan was nowhere to be found. His parents finally located him behind the house, crying his heart out. When they asked him to come in for the meal, he refused. It was a long time before Ervan wanted to drive the truck again.

As for Paul, he didn't suffer any permanent damage from the accident. However, he did stutter a lot as a child, and I have always wondered if his speech impediment could have resulted from his being run over. One of the family said that little Paul, in surviving the accident, was as strong as Popeye. The name stuck; even today Paul is "Popeye" to his friends.

During those pre-school years I again disobeyed Dad one day. The act of disobedience has long since been forgotten, but not what followed. Feeling very guilty, and being sure that a spanking was called for, I decided to hide. Casting about for a secure place of seclusion, I spied the corn crib. The floor of this narrow building was just high enough off the ground for me to crawl under. Some kind of screen effectively hid me.

After my long hours of guilt, dampness, and loneliness, Dad came home. It was supper time, and Mother made her usual call from the back door. When I didn't respond, the search was on. Dad first looked around the barn and other farm buildings. Then Mother helped in the search. When the situation became serious, Uncle Jonas and Aunt Lizzie, who lived in the other house, joined in the hunt for the lost boy.

Dad came to the corn crib and looked inside a number of times. When he walked past, his feet were so close I could have reached out and touched them. His frantic calls of "Paul, where are you?" echo across the years and stir up feelings of guilt even yet.

"But then," as Dad enjoyed telling the story, "Paul got careless and made a mistake. He started to move a small board back and forth, and the end of that board stuck past the end of the crib. I saw the board moving and decided there must be a boy on the other end!"

Suddenly Dad was on his hands and knees, peering into the dark interior of my hiding place. "Paul, are you in there?"

My only reply was a sob.

"Come out right now," said Dad, far more gently than I could have expected. I came crawling out, dirty and fearful.

Was I spanked and sent off to bed without supper? No. In fact, I don't remember being scolded. The atmosphere at the supper table was one of great rejoicing. Perhaps that day's happenings provide the background which causes Christ's story of the prodigal son to always move me deeply. I suspect that such childhood experiences convey the love of our heavenly father much more effectively than years of teaching and preaching.

Twenty-two years later I had a similar experience. Our daughter, Karen, was also disobedient, and also hid. We lived in town, and before long the whole neighborhood joined in our panic and search. But to no avail. We finally gave up as it was getting dark and decided to call the police.

We were talking about this as we returned to our house. "Here I am!" came a small, squeaky voice from behind a large shrub beside our front door.

Did we punish her? Foolish question! We scolded her with love and hugs. And from that time on I can better appreciate the story of the prodigal son from the Father perspective.

Dad's carrot story also came out of the muck farm years. When the truck-garden vegetables such as radishes, lettuce, turnips, onions, and carrots were brought in from the fields, the next step in getting them ready for the farmers market was washing and packaging. A large steel tank was filled almost to capacity with water and a basket or two of produce dumped in.

After they were allowed to soak a bit, the vegetables were swished around vigorously to dislodge most of the dirt. A brush was then used to remove any remaining soil.

One day Dad was working alone in this washing-shed. He

44

was feeling especially good as he meditated on the blessings he had received from the Lord. As he washed carrots for the next day's market, he sang a few lines of a gospel song. Now, Dad did two things when singing which greatly irritated better singers. First, he was slightly off pitch. And secondly, he sang a line or so of a given song, paused a moment, and then sang the same phrase over and over again.

Although this drove some listeners to distraction, Dad had a great time as he worked with his hands along with exercising his vocal cords.

On this day he was washing the carrots, tossing them into baskets, and singing something like, "We shall come rejoicing, Bringing in the sheaves." As he worked, he threw all crooked carrots into the bottom of the next basket to be filled. In that way, all baskets had beautiful, straight ones on top. This, incidentally, was the way everyone in the business did it.

Having filled another basket, Dad was setting it aside when he noticed a crooked carrot which had escaped his attention and ended up on top. So he reached for a replacement. Just as his hand plunged into the water, God's Spirit checked him. "Hiding the crooked carrots is dishonest and not pleasing to me."

Dad was stunned. He had never thought of it that way. Everyone was doing it; even the buyers knew that.

But Dad obeyed the promptings of the Spirit. Typical of his exuberance as a young Christian, he swung over to the other extreme and placed the crooked carrots on the top of the baskets! "Bringing in the sheaves" was sung with more volume and joy than ever.

The next day at market a lady bought a peck of carrots and asked Dad to empty the basket into her own container in order to save the cost of the basket. Expecting to see a poorer grade of carrots now on top, she was amazed to discover only fine straight ones. Highly pleased, she exclaimed, "You put the best ones in the *bottom* of the basket!"

When Dad told her why, the lady was impressed. "I'll be back again." She became a regular customer, and the sound of music produced by Dad the next time he washed carrots was beyond description. As someone said, "He had a rich voice—always well off!"

My sister, Evangeline, was born in the farmhouse of the muck farm in the spring of 1931, the sixth child. The great depression was in full swing and truck farming suffered along with everything else.

Dad was ready to roll again.

45

Chapter 8

CIDER PRESS WHEELS

Move Number Eight was to another farm nearer North Lawrence and also nearer the Sippo Church. Dad farmed some of the land but ventured into a new occupation—the hatchery business. He bought a large incubator which almost filled one room of the rented farmhouse and began hatching baby-chicks. The little peeps were cute and a lot of fun, but they were also a lot of work for a lad of seven.

To further supplement the income, Dad used the truck which he had brought from the farm to do custom hauling. In warm weather we children were allowed to ride atop the loads, and was it ever fun! In fall months much of the trucking involved wheat, loaded from the fields and taken directly to the mills in Massillon.

He also hauled coal. One day he brought a load to the small one-room schoolhouse about a mile from our home. Classes were in session when Dad drove in. I stood up at my seat to look out, and then said in a louder than intended whisper, "That's my DAD out there!" The recitations in another grade stopped, and the teacher looked at me in amusement.

As some of the children started to snicker, Miss Mackey noted my embarrassment and quickly said, "That is Paul's dad out there and I'm very glad he came today. We are almost out of coal." I sat down, grateful for her thoughtfulness.

We boys desperately wanted a bicycle, but no money was available for even a used one. One day we found the frame of an adult-size bike on a junk pile and brought it home to Dad. He looked it over and allowed that he might be able to put wheels on it. We hunted through barn and sheds and found two wheels, one about eight inches in diameter and the other around ten.

Dad mounted the wheels on the old frame with the small one at the rear. The bike had no seat, so we wrapped rags around the bars to provide a small degree of comfort. Lloyd and I spent many hours with that pedal-less bike, pushing each other up hills and then climbing on for the ride down together.

Then one wonderful day Dad came home with a sparkling new red bicycle. The wheels were sixteen inches in diameter, and the pedals were for real even though they were on the front wheel. And it had a *seat*. Mother protested that it cost too much, but her smile cancelled out her words.

In keeping with what was by now a family tradition, another baby was born at this new location. A boy, he arrived in the spring of 1933 when the depression was at its deepest. They named their seventh child George, in honor of his Grandfather Yoder, and Washington, in honor of another important man. George Washington Hostetler—who could fail with a name like that? (In his adult years, George has discreetly reduced the Washington to a W.)

A woman who came to buy baby-chicks at the hatchery asked Mother how many children she had. She replied that her sixth living child had been born not long before and then introduced me as the eldest of the family. The woman carefully looked me over—skinny, small for my age, eight years old—and then turned to Mother. "I'm sure you wanted each one of them."

Mother was surprised. "Why, of course we wanted each one!" It was a completely new thought to me. What other kind of children are there, I wondered? Not long afterwards I learned.

Taking care of all the children and helping Dad in the fields and hatchery was getting to be too much for Mother to handle. In their contacts with the Brethren in Christ Church at large, they heard of an orphanage near Mount Joy, Pennsylvania. Upon inquiring, they learned about a twelve year old girl from a broken home. Dad and Mother made the long trip to Pennsylvania that summer and came home with Grace Sliger.

Mother often said that Grace was a gift to our home from the hand of God. How different it must have looked at first from the eyes and heart of the young lass. The difficulty of facing and then being integrated into a family of eight must have been almost overwhelming. But Grace was industrious and large-hearted. She succeeded where most would have failed.

She washed clothes and dishes and bodies and floors. She soon put us young urchins in place with firm hand and stick when necessary. And she delighted her foster-parents' hearts with her beautiful singing voice. Before long she and Mother were much in demand to sing duets at our home church and in the many revival meetings we were always attending.

Grace was a much loved part of our family until she met and married Earl Rohrer, a fine young Christian from the Valley Chapel Brethren in Christ Church near Canton, Ohio.

Mother contracted measles in 1933 and became very ill. She was so low that Dad called in Christian friends to pray with him. We older children came to her bedside, keenly aware that she might be dying. I had the sickening feelings of the days of Mary Ellen's sickness, death, and funeral. This is the only time I remember Mother ever being ill. She was probably sick at other times, but mothers are so much needed when their children are young that they seldom let sickness get them down.

Times were getting a bit better as President Franklin Roosevelt brought in the National Recovery Act and many other progressive political moves to get the country back on its feet again. The year was 1934, and Dad was once again looking toward greener pastures.

He purchased an old one-room brick schoolhouse just a mile north of North Lawrence, right at the top of a hill. Since the big room had a feedmill in it, Dad decided to move the house which he and Uncle Jonas had built on the muck farm to this place. It was a two-story building, about sixteen feet wide and thirty-six feet long.

How to transport it to the new location two miles away was a problem. Dad solved it by hiring a large tractor-trailer rig and getting plenty of planks and jacks. The house was gradually levered up until the huge trailer could be backed underneath. The first part of the move was the most precarious because the house was built on a slope. In order to keep the house from tilting too much in that first pull, ropes were fastened to the top and about ten men stationed at the other end of the ropes on the uphill side.

When all was ready, Dad gave the signal to the driver. The house slowly began to move. When the wheels of the truck came to the worst part of the slope, the house lurched alarmingly, throwing many of the men off their feet. Some let their ropes fly. A neighbor yelled, "She's going to tip over!"

One side of the house lifted off the flat bed of the truck and teetered there for an agonizing moment. "Pull!" bellowed Dad. The men who still held ropes gave an adrenalin-inspired heave. The house settled slowly back into place.

It was a great day for boys but rather wearing on dads!

The building was hauled uneventfully up the road and placed against the gable end of the schoolhouse with one end extending about twenty feet beyond. Dad then added an ell to the 20-foot section, resulting in a wrap-around effect.

Not long afterward, Dad moved the feedmill out of the schoolhouse and into a large addition he built on the side opposite the house we lived in. The incubator was placed in the schoolhouse. Because of the high ceiling, two stories were built into about half the large schoolroom, and battery brooders installed. Dad was then in the hatchery, broiler, and feedmill business.

The income for all these, however, was not enough to keep food on the table. Dad therefore built another addition to the addition which housed the feedmill and brought in a huge cider press. This provided good cash in the fall months, but there was a problem. Dad was bothered by the fact that some people who had juice squeezed from their apples, pears, or grapes, talked with enthusiasm about the "joy" the beverages would bring them later.

Dad prayed about this and finally came to the difficult decision that he could no longer press fruit for those who had such intentions. The word spread around the community. Thenceforth the errant guzzlers either reformed or else kept their sinful plans and habits to themselves.

In setting up the cider press, Dad devised a conglomeration of shafts, pulleys, and belts complicated enough to bring pleasure to the heart of any mechanic. We boys drank sweet cider every fall day and ate the apples which Dad selected from the customers' many bushels with their approval. He lined these up on a shelf during the day to await our hungry arrival after the one-mile walk from school.

The huge maple beams between the large screws and the ground-up apples being pressed were cracked with age. As tons of pressure were put upon them, the cracks would shift with resounding bangs. It was fun to watch people jump in fright.

One day Dad went up the stairs and onto the walkways among the machinery to replace a belt which had slipped off. As he reached for the belt, he failed to notice a bolt in the coupling which fastened the two parts of the long lineshaft together.

Suddenly one trouser leg of his almost-new blue denim bib overalls caught on the bolt. At almost the same time the other trouser leg also became entangled. As he stood there helplessly, the shaft viciously tore his pants off, pulling his legs tightly against the abrasive rust.

In moments his new overalls were nothing but a blur of whirling denim. Dad's first concern was that the women standing below might look up and see him in his exposed circumstances. So he hurried to the steps on the other side of the room, stumbled down, and ran for the house.

Dad took a real beating that day. He had ugly bruises on both shoulders where the strong suspenders had been ripped off. His shins required many weeks of salving and wrapping before they healed. He carried the scars of his dreadful mistake from that day on. At family prayers, Dad often thanked the Lord that his life had been spared.

When we talked about this in later years, we amused ourselves and Dad by suggesting that the women standing below him probably got an eyefull. Dad would say, "Now boys, you shouldn't think such unkind things about your old dad!" And then he would rethink the terrible moments. "But I tell you something. If they got a look, they didn't see much of anything because I set a new speed record for getting out of a cider press!"

And one of us would mimic him by saying, "Isn't that the berries! I yi yi yi yi! For pity sakes!"

The left-overs from the apple-squeezings were called apple-pummies, according to Dad. Neither dictionary nor encyclopedia yields any clue on this word. However, "pummies" seems to be such a correct word for the gooey stuff. So pummies it is.

The pummies accumulated and had to be hauled away. Dad bought a Jiffy-Dump truck for this chore. The steel bed of the Model-T Ford truck was mounted high and fastened on a pivot just forward of center. In that way, when a lever was pulled, the bed would tip quickly and dump its load in a jiffy.

In the year that I was twelve Dad allowed me to drive the Model-T. Dad's hired hand at the time was Ben Troyer. Now, one thing that Dad wouldn't tolerate in his hired help was tobacco smoking. All of us suspected that Ben was smoking on the sly, but we had no proof.

One day we were hauling pummies to a farm a few miles away. Ben insisted on riding on the load rather than in the cab with me. This was fine until I noticed by his shadow beside the truck as we drove along that he appeared to be smoking. Solid evidence was needed, so I leaned out the window and stretched around the cab. And I caught him in the very act.

The next thing I knew the Jiffy-Dump was off the road, careening through a shallow ditch, and charging into a cornfield. Mercifully, we managed to miss everything except a large corn shock. Ben shouted and the corn flew! After we skidded to a stop, he jumped off the truck and said some choice words designed to make me a more careful driver.

He interspersed his scoldings with vigorous puffs on his coffin nail. When he saw me looking at the offending weed, his sermonizing ended. We stood face to face, both guilty of unacceptable deeds which Dad would surely reward with a revoked driving privilege on the one hand, and a lost job on the other.

A calculating look came into Ben's eyes. "Let's not tell anyone about this," he proposed. I solemnly agreed. We set up the banged-down corn shock, cleaned the evidence out of Jiffey's radiator, and went our way.

Not many days later Dad himself caught Ben smoking and told him to light his fires elsewhere. The day he said goodbye was Ben's chance to tell on me. But he didn't. He may have been a smoker, but he wasn't a squealer.

Chapter 9

BIG WHEELS

Dad and Mother brought up their children to be respectful during church services, but some of us were slow learners. With a sizable brood to watch, they just couldn't monitor all successfully.

Someone in our crowd of boys at church introduced the idea of shooting paper wads with rubber bands. We were really stinging each other in an evening service. The most fun was when we started bouncing them off a couple of bald heads within striking range. The men would look angrily around, only to be met with looks of angelic innocence.

I thought we had launched our missiles without being detected until after church when Mother promptly informed me that we three boys would get a licking as soon as we got home. Even Dad, who was always more mild mannered, was clearly upset. Mother, who usually needed to administer spankings because Dad chickened out, saw that this was a good time for Dad to have the honors.

He took me and my two brothers, Lloyd and Eli Jr., into our bedroom. He was squeamish and we were scared. "Now, before I spank you," he began, "I would like to say a few things." He then said how disappointed he was with our behavior and wondered where he had gone wrong in rearing us.

Then he just sat there and cried. It was awful. Since the licking was surely coming, why didn't he stop the sobs and start the swats? After what seemed like a very long time he regained control of his emotions, but he just sat quietly with bowed head. We three boys looked at each other uneasily.

Finally he looked up and instructed us to kneel by the bedside, all of us. I can remember wondering if Dad had devised some new procedure of hitting bottoms three at a time. As we trembled in that exposed position, Dad knelt behind us, put his hands on our shoulders, and prayed. He prayed for each of us by name, and then prayed for wisdom to give

52

proper guidance to his boys.

When he finished, Dad pulled us to our feet and said gruffly, "The next time you boys shoot paper wads in church, I am personally going to use the stick on you! Now get yourselves ready for bed."

We watched through a crack in the door as he rejoined Mother. "It didn't sound to me like you gave the boys a very hard licking; I didn't hear them crying." (We were usually great with sound effects!) Dad admitted that he had used other means of discipline and looked sheepish—until Mother smiled.

As for us boys, we wanted no part of that kind of discipline. A good solid spanking was much better. A stinging bottom was much preferred to a praying session.

Dad's method was 100 percent effective. His boys never shot paper wads in church again.

I started in the fourth grade in the North Lawrence school. The building had four rooms but only three were used for classrooms because the other was condemned as being unsafe. Ironically, that room was used as a small gymnasium in which we played volleyball. It withstood repeated jumping and thumping, and regretably never collapsed.

The principal, Mr. Troxel, was rather literature-minded and instituted two literary societies in the school, dividing the eight grades equally. He had a literary program the last hour of school, once a month. Dad did not allow us to participate in the programs, but his compromise was that we could attend.

One fateful day the program featured one of the students as a tap dancer, clad in a very scanty costume. We older ones knew better than let Dad know about this, but a guileless younger member let it slip out, and it was a lot worse than the berries! Dad went to see Mr. Troxel and asked to have his children excused from future literary programs. When the principal refused, Dad simply kept us all out of school the next time.

Mr. Troxel played his trump card. He called the truant officer in the county seat, Canton, and he came to see Dad the same day.

When Dad refused to let us go to school, the officer, who had what looked like a very large gun in a holster under his coat, told Dad that he would need to return to Canton with him. As they drove away, our childish fears imagined all kinds of terrible judgments being pronounced upon Dad, including his execution.

A few hours later the truant officer brought Dad back home and he was still alive. What is more, he was smiling. The county school superintendent in Canton had listened to Dad's story with sympathy and ruled that he should present his case to the local school board.

When the regular board meeting date came around, Dad went to the meeting, taking me along. Pretty heavy stuff for a fourth grader! Dad told about the tap dancer, and the board chairman almost had a heart attack. "Do they call that a literary program?" he sputtered in anger. He cussed until he noticed that my eyes were bulging and my mouth hanging open!

The board made two rulings. First, no more dancing at literary programs. And second, Dad's children could be excused from the programs if they behaved themselves in another room. And that took care of that.

A year and a half after we moved to the house on the hill, another son was born into the family. The eighth child, Dad and Mother named him Albert Glenn soon after he first saw daylight on a cold January day in 1936.

My oldest cousin, Callista Hostetler, was being married that summer, and all of us were invited to the wedding. When the honored guests were being seated at the reception, Dad and two other relatives who had also left the Amish Church were seated at the long, main table.

One of the preachers saw them there and informed my Uncle Dan, father of the bride, that the three men would need to be moved to another table before he would be seated. He took this position because of his church's interpretation of the Bible verse found in II Corinthians 6:17: "Wherefore come out from among them, and be ye separate, saith the Lord, and touch not the unclean thing."

Uncle Dan was a kind man and wouldn't have hurt the feelings of anyone if he could at all help it. But the protesting preacher was one of the officiating ministers in the wedding. It was a dreadful dilemma, but Uncle Dan finally found in favor of the protester. He shamefacedly came to Dad and the other two men and asked them to be seated at another table.

Dad was not at all pleased, but he allowed himself to be

seated elsewhere. The other two shunees, however, were not as amicable. They stalked out of the house, got into a car, raced the motor, and tore up the turf on their way to dinner at a restaurant.

Dad managed to have the last laugh, and how he enjoyed telling about it. From his "lower" seat in another room, he could see through the doorway that the objecting minister was seated in the very place Dad had occupied. It was a hot day, and Dad had taken a drink of water as soon as he sat down. When victorious Brother Shunner sat down, he looked around in triumph and took a drink of water from the very glass Dad had desecrated only moments before!

As Dad would reflect on the day, he pointed out to us that three parties had done wrong, maybe four. The two wheel-spinning relatives were the worst, then the shunning preacher, then Uncle Dan for going against his own desires because of pressure—and perhaps even Dad himself for feeling good about the water glass.

After dinner the younger generation also got into the shunning spirit. We lined up on sides and shouted insults across no man's land. It was pretty much a verbal standoff like Saul and Goliath of Old Testament times until one of my cousins, Harold Helmuth, became our David. He grabbed another bigger cousin and gave him a sound licking.

All in all, it was one of the most exciting wedding receptions I ever attended.

Chapter 10

FEED MILL WHEELS

Soon after we moved to the hilltop place Dad began to pray fervently that God would send more laborers into the harvest field. He often had this burden at the family altar. One morning as Dad was praying, God suddenly seemed to appear and point his finger at him. Dad was so startled that he stopped praying.

The next morning at family prayer time he again prayed the same prayer, and again he had the vision of God standing before him with a stern finger pointed right at him. Again he stopped praying. Then he told Mother what was happening.

"I don't see how I can become a preacher," he argued. "Right now I am hatching chicks, raising broilers, grinding feed, pressing apples, and farming. And even then I can hardly make ends meet."

Mother was sympathetic. She was helping to get bills paid, even with all her young children, by doing practical nursing in area homes. But she wanted Dad to do God's will. It was a terrific struggle. Reason and circumstances said no. But in the end Dad obeyed God's call.

Once each month our family was attending a small church called Geyer's Chapel, some twenty-five miles west of North Lawrence. A few Brethren in Christ members lived in the area and worshiped with the United Brethren at the chapel.

When the good people there learned about Dad's struggle, they talked to their pastor, and he promptly asked Dad to preach the next time he came. A month later Dad preached his first sermon. Before long he was asked to preach at the Sippo Church. He was ordained to the ministry in the Brethren in Christ Church in 1935, and his name appeared on the church's roster of active ministers the next year.

Our family continued to attend Geyer's Chapel for quite a number of years. When I, then Lloyd, and then Eli Jr. also felt called to the ministry in our late teens, each of us in turn preached his first sermon at the same church.

A handful of years have gone by since then. I recently made a pilgrimage to the site of the little country chapel. To my dismay, only green grass and flowers covered the place where the church once stood. I climbed out of the car and walked to what must have been very near the spot where the pulpit had been. My wife clicked a shutter while my mind spanned the years.

As I stood there in the well kept lawn, I thanked God for the loving and long-suffering saints who were willing to let a father and his three sons each try out his homiletic wings in their midst as they prayed and nodded encouragement.

The cemetery was nearby. I walked among the stones and tried to remember the name of the aged woman who was my Sunday School teacher during my boyhood years at Geyer's Chapel. She made a profound impression on me for good. Always praying for every child in the class by name each Sunday, she assured us that she did the same every morning and evening of every single day. You know, it is reassuring to a growing boy when he is being prayed for every day by his own parents, and fourteen extra times a week by his teacher.

The Sippo Church had a "multiple ministry." Dad was one of three preachers in the small congregation of less than a hundred people. All three supported themselves with other occupations. Willie J. Meyers was the head minister, and the third pastor was Joe Slabaugh in the early years and Marion Berg later on.

I rated them in this order: Berg, Slabaugh, Myers, and Dad. The rating was based strictly on length of sermon. Many adults, I suspect, tend to rate sermons the same way.

Dad told good stories in his sermons, but he got carried away with enthusiasm and often preached all of half an hour. That is a long confinement for a boy itching to get out into the sun or snow. Bishop Myers always cried a lot when he preached, and his tears made me uncomfortable. Adults sometimes called him the weeping prophet; we children called him Weeping Willie when no adults were around.

Joe Slabaugh generally preached for twenty minutes, a great improvement over Pastor Myers and Dad. Reverend Berg, however, was best of all. When he preached his usual 15-minute sermon, we could count on getting out of church by 11:15.

57

His name brings to mind a funny thing that happened one Sunday just as he was bringing his short sermon to a close. Dad punctuated other preachers' sermons with enthusiastic "Amens" or "That's right, brother," when he agreed with what was being proclaimed. Well, on this Sunday Dad did something he rarely did in church and just never did when sitting in the pulpit—he went to sleep.

I watched him uneasily, but he managed to neither snore nor fall off the seat. Then, just as Pastor Berg was winding up his sermon, Dad began to show signs of stirring. Said Pastor Berg, "I guess it's time to bring this sermon to a close."

At that precise moment Dad's eyes blinked open. Obviously embarrassed, and rather sure that he was behind schedule on responding to the preaching, he immediately injected his tardy "Amen, brother!"

Preacher Berg was stunned and the congregation gasped. Dad's encouraging words practically unhinged the Gospel messenger! He sputtered to his conclusion about as coherently as a man with his mouth full of mashed potatoes.

Now, in those multiple ministry days the preachers not giving the sermon were always expected to make appropriate comments when the speaker sat down. Accordingly, when Pastor Berg took his seat, Dad was on. Not only was he shaken because of having fallen asleep before the whole congregation, he now needed to respond to a sermon the most of which he hadn't heard.

Dad struggled to his feet. He said some mighty fine things which in no way related to the sermon. When he sat down, Pastor Myers tried to salvage the situation, but to no avail. I wonder if Pastor Berg had unhappy vibrations toward Dad for a long time afterward. If so, I don't blame him a bit. Dad should have stayed in bed that Sunday!

Our whole family always attended the midweek prayer meeting. People who didn't attend were more or less relegated to the ranks of the backsliders. In those days, the thirties, the brothers and sisters knelt for prayer, and the leader usually called for a "season" of prayer.

Believe me, those seasons of prayer were long, long seasons. It was nothing unusual for children to fall asleep if they weren't busy crawling under the benches or engaged in some other form of mischief. And the children were always there. Baby sitters were unheard of in our circles.

Once in a while an adult dozed off. This was much frowned on because the real saints were hanging in there by either praying out loud or giving their assent every once in a while with a hearty "Amen" or "Do it, Lord."

One night a weary saint dozed off even before the season of prayer was called for. When all the people knelt, the sleeping brother simply stayed sitting. He was very visible because most everyone else was below the level of the pew backs.

Except that the young people present were laying mental wagers on when he would awaken, nothing more happened during the prayer time. All was well until the leader signaled the end of the prayer season with a resigned "let us rise" after no one had prayed for a while. In the scuffling of shoes as the faithful ones resumed their seats, dear Brother Slumber was finally aroused.

He was confused, thinking he had fallen asleep on his knees as had happened before. So he decided to get up along with everyone else. But he was already sitting up. In his daze, he put his feet up on the seat of the pew and sat on the backrest. The look on his face when he slowly realized where he was perched was both pathetic and comical.

Slumber quickly plopped into his proper seat, and the benediction followed soon after! That is one of the notable prayer meetings of my boyhood. I do distinctly remember one more.

We were again engaged in a long season of prayer. The cold winter weather caused me to choose one of the three benches which surrounded the pot-bellied stove in the old Sippo Church. As I was kneeling there, a lad of eleven or twelve, I heard someone moving stealthily toward me. Looking around, I saw Dad coming on his hands and knees, taking care to keep his head low.

He was coming to me from a distance of about one-fourth a small church. Had he gone off his rocker? When he arrived at my side he whispered gently, "Paul, I would be very pleased if you would lead in a short prayer next." I just quietly shook my head. He waited a bit, and I noticed a tear on his cheek.

As the good brother who was praying continued, bless him, my father crawled back to his place. No one ever knew what he had done until I revealed it years later. Even as I am writing this, I can see his sharply defined face in the flickering light of the open stove door, at first so hopeful, and then so disappointed.

Soon after we moved to the place on the hill, Dad decided to dig out a basement under the feedmill wing and part of the schoolhouse itself. He used a neighbor's horse and slip-scraper. The scraper had a cutting edge at the front and two handles at the back. When handled with skill, the scraper would dig as the horse pulled, loading itself in much the same manner as modern earth movers. When *not* handled with skill, the slipscraper would tilt suddenly forward, throwing the operator over the handles.

Starting in at the north side of the feedmill building, we gradually dug our way under it and then on under the schoolhouse. Care was taken to stay about four feet away from the foundations to make sure they didn't collapse.

The hard work was completed after many days, and Dad moved the hammermill and Ford V-8 engine which powered it into the new cellar. He attached extended controls on the ignition, starter, throttle, choke, gearshift, and clutch so that the motor and mill could be operated from the floor above.

The fuel for the engine was stored in a large tank outside the building. Dad trusted everyone and therefore didn't keep it locked. Enterprising thieves noticed the unsecured tank and helped themselves to the gas. After this happened a number of times, Dad decided to take corrective action.

First, he allowed the feedmill engine to use up all the gas in the tank and then hooked its fuel line to another hidden tank. He then filled the big fuel tank with the garden hose. The next morning all the water was still in the tank. Same thing the following morning. But on the fourth night the gas-stealers were back again while we were gone to church. They either had more than one car or else had extra containers with them because they spirited away many gallons.

The new kind of petrol must have been unusually long-lasting. The thieves never came back again.

The man who brought the fuel in his large truck was the same driver who had been bringing Dad gasoline and kerosene from my earliest memory of the muck farm days. Somehow he managed to get lost when making a delivery somewhere, and Dad told us about it. From that day on we children dubbed him John-Gone-the-Wrong-Way.

In those farm days we would put stones under the wheels of John-Gone-the-Wrong-Way's truck in an attempt to stall his engine. When we did this he would chase us, yelling all kinds of imprecations acceptable to boyish or parental ears. And he would scare us terribly every time! Only in later years did I realize John enjoyed the whole ritual.

One day John-Gone-the-Wrong-Way again caught us placing stones under his wheels. He decided to chase me, shouting that the results would be dire indeed if he caught me. I tore across the lawn with John in hot pursuit, looking back over my shoulder.

My looking back, like the Bible man not acceptable for the Kingdom, was also my undoing. My path of flight veered, and I ran smack into a tree at top speed. Now, that is the kind of activity out of which stars are born! John-Gone-the-Wrong-Way quickly picked me up and headed for our house, anxiously calling, "Mrs. Hostetler! Mrs. Hostetler!"

His red-faced explanation to Mother would have been funny if my head hadn't been aching so much. Mother quickly brushed aside any need for apologies. She had been observing his game with us boys for some time.

Chapter 11

MODEL-A FORD WHEELS

Dad loved to preach evangelistic sermons. In the winter of 1936-37 he was invited to preach for a revival meeting in Orlando, Florida. He accepted the invitation from the Brethren in Christ Church there, and furthermore, decided to take his whole family with him.

In preparation for the trip he built a small house-trailer to pull behind the '29 Model-A Ford panel truck we had at the time. When one considers how poor the brakes were on the truck, and the fact that the trailer had none at all, it is some kind of miracle that we survived the adventure.

I was in the sixth grade, Lloyd in the fifth, Eli Jr. in the fourth, and Lois in the second. Evangeline was almost five, George almost three, and Albert turned one year old the day we left, January 2, 1937. Grace was also along.

Because of the size of the family, some rode in the truck (henceforth called a van for convenience) and the rest in the trailer. In order to assure needed communication between van and trailer, Dad devised a buzzer system backed up with a hose.

The buzzer was used for simple messages and to signal that the receiving party should get his ear to the hose. The most often used signals were: one buzz for Number 1 and two buzzes for Number 2, parallel with the system used at school when raised fingers sought permission from the teacher for a trip to the outdoor toilets.

With seven children on board, Dad and Mother were badgered with the frantic buzzings, necessitating frequent pit stops. They finally dispatched the most frequent violators, mostly the younger ones, to the trailer with Mother or one of us older children in charge. The trailer had no restroom, but behind a curtain it did have a container (euphemistically called a chamber vessel).

Three buzzes meant "I want to talk to someone," and four

meant "I am hungry," etc. It was a great system, and we children whiled away many hours saying such things as "How long until we stop?" and other equally imaginative conversation. When we wanted the listening person to get the hose from his ear to his mouth, we simply quit talking and started listening. We hadn't heard of the convenient "Over" or "10-4" used today.

Consequently, both people at times had their ear to the hose, and sometimes both were talking at once. It made for a lot of confusion, but who cared—we were headed for the Sunshine State! As we moved along in van and trailer, we sang a song which we had learned in school.

We're going down south! Way, way down south,
    Where the sun shines every day.
Bright skies of blue, smile down on you,
    And all the birds are singing clear and gay.
Come on along, join in the song,
    Hop on board, it won't be long.
We're on our way—hip, hip hurray!
    We're going down south today!

I haven't sung the song in forty years, but the words and music are easily recalled.

We crossed the Ohio River at Cincinnati. Barely across the bridge into Covington, Kentucky, the frightening sound of a police siren caused Dad to pull over to the side. Two officers got out and, without saying a word, began to measure our rig from stem to stern. They then informed Dad that we were in violation of the law.

The State of Kentucky was unhappy with the big tractor-trailer trucks going through the state without buying fuel and therefore avoiding the payment of tax. A law was enacted making it illegal for any such vehicle to cross the state if longer than so many feet. Our little van and trailer were just a few feet too long. If the van had been a car, we would not have been stopped regardless of length.

Dad was taken away to the Justice of the Peace and informed the fine was $50. "Fifty dollars," he exclaimed in dismay, "that's all I have in my pocket!" He then told the justice that he and his family were on their way to Florida but wouldn't even be able to buy enough gas to get back home if he paid the $50 fine.

The lawman chopped the fine in half; he didn't want to have ten people on his hands. Dad tried to get a further reduction, but to no avail. All this time we were sitting at the roadside, wondering what was happening. When the officers brought Dad back, we all got into the van to hear his story. He and Mother then needed to make a decision on whether to continue south or return home.

Finally Dad said, "Let's pray about this." As he prayed, I tried to discern whether it was go or stay. I was praying a little prayer of my own that it would be the former. When his prayer ended, he informed us that we would trust in God and travel on toward Florida. We children greeted his good news with a shout of approval! But Dad was in no shouting mood as he slowly started the motor and pulled the shift lever into low.

With the funds so severely depleted, providing three meals a day took some doing. As I recall, we had plenty of food, but it consisted mainly of bread, pancakes, potatoes, and soda crackers.

The next crisis was a broken rear spring on the van in Georgia. After thumping along for a few miles, we pulled into an overnight camping place about midday. Dad went to a local "junk yard" and bought a used spring. He then borrowed jacks and we went to work with the good tools he had brought along "just in case." The weather was warm and our workshop was on a flat, grassy area. It was hard, dirty work, but the spring was in place by the time the sun went down.

The next day we arrived at the Florida state line. The first thing we noticed was a huge pile of oranges near the inspection station. Dad learned that a trucker had been caught trying to smuggle uninspected fruit across the border and was forced to dump his whole load on the ground. Boy, those oranges looked good to kids who got very little fresh fruit in the wintertime!

When Dad asked for oranges for his hungry family, the officer said it was against the regulations. But then he looked around our circle of pleading eyes and said, "If I don't see you when you take some, how can I do anything about it?" After warning us to be sure no one else saw us, he gave us a big box and turned his back. We quickly filled the box to overflowing and were soon on our way. All talk ceased for many miles as we schlurped the juicy carriers of Vitamin C.

Florida proved to be a land of sunshine and Orlando was

beautiful to behold with its more than thirty lakes inside the city limits. We found the church where Rev. Floyd Winger was the pastor. He showed us where to park the trailer in the lawn behind the church and helped us pitch a tent which he supplied.

In a few days the evangelistic meetings started, continuing for the next two weeks. During all those days we children played under the palms and wandered through nearby orange groves. Oranges, tangerines, and grapefruit were easy to buy at from twenty to forty cents a bushel. We went fishing in the lakes. With school books and cold weather left far behind, it seemed that we were living in some sort of preliminary heaven.

A school for black college students was located not far from Orlando. Every Sunday afternoon their excellent choir gave a concert, drawing large crowds from miles around. Dad took our family over to hear the singers. They were good, very good. From the first Sunday on we went each week. I suppose one reason was that admission was free.

One perennial favorite sung by all the men in the choir as the final selection in each program was "The Train Song." They lined up from one end of the platform to the other, facing toward the audience left. Each one grasped the elbow of the one in front of him, and all arms swung back and forth together in time with the music, looking very much like the huge drive shafts on the mighty steam locomotives which pulled trains in those times. Then they would sing:

Dis train is bound for glory, dis train, my Lord,
Dis train is bound for glory, dis train, my Lord,
Dis train is bound for glory—all who go must be holy,
Lord, Lord, Lord, dis train.

Then they paused while the first in line reached up to "blow the whistle," a harmonious waaa-unk, waa-unk, wank, wank, waaa-unk. Then the next verse:

Dis train don't carry no gamblers, dis train my Lord,
(repeat)
Dis train don't carry no gamblers—no hoboes nor midnight ramblers!
Lord, Lord, Lord—dis train.

Waaa-unk, etc.

Other verses were: Dis train don't carry no loafers, no snuff-dippers nor tobacco smokers! and, Dis train don't carry no sinners, no big fish that swaller minners!

The final stanza was a repeat of the first with one difference; the singers started it very slowly, keeping in time with arms and feet, and moving off stage. As the verse went on, the train picked up speed. When the verse ended the train was going full speed, and the crowd was standing to their feet with a "right on" ovation.

Without ever seeing the words or music to the Train Song, my two brothers and I began to sing it in three part harmony. In the next few years until my voice changed, we sang the song (and many others of less distinction) in revival meetings and conventions many, many times. Dad and Mother were always there, so proud of their sons it bordered on sinfulness. They must have lain awake at night figuring out new frontiers to conquer in the music world.

When the two weeks of the Florida meeting were over, Dad discovered that the honorarium he received for preaching, although as generous as could be expected, barely covered his day to day expenses while in Florida. So he looked around for employment. Pastor Winger had the answer; he was building a house which needed lathing. Dad contracted the job. The trick was to nail the small wood laths on all the joists and studs of the interior ceilings and walls, leaving a small space between each one.

Long before that two-week job was over we boys were anxious to leave the land of balmy breezes. Our preliminary heaven had deteriorated into a purgatory of bruised thumbs and slivered fingers. From that day to this, I haven't been able to look at a plaster lath in kindness!

When Dad suggested we head for home, no objections were raised. It was now almost six weeks since we left Ohio. A lady in Florida proposed that we go home by way of Harrisburg, Pennsylvania, and take her along to help pay the expenses. It would add more days to our trip, but Dad agreed to do this. It was a sad mistake. She was old and crochety, and always managed to have a headache which forced us children to tread and speak softly.

What a drag.

The second day out of Florida we drove close to a lake where many were fishing. Our family needed a break and seriously considered putting lines in the water, but Mrs. Crochety frowned away the idea.

We finally arrived in Washington D.C. and decided to see the sights. We went to the top of the slender, sky-stabbing obelisk dedicated to the memory of our first president while Mrs. Crochety sulked. We visited the Lincoln Memorial, Mount Vernon, and a few other places, with our guest refusing to get out of the van. Our noisy family had gotten to be too much for her.

Our next stop was the newly completed Messiah Old People's Home (as then called) in Harrisburg. Mrs. Crochety parted from our company there with a sigh of relief on the part of everyone.

The next morning we headed west on the final 300-mile leg of our long trip. As we travelled along mountainous Route 22, Dad got too near the edge of the highway on a curve, and the right rear wheel of the van dropped off the pavement. He kept the van and trailer under control, but the wheel began to wobble and finally broke, puncturing the tire.

As we had done a number of times on the trip, the family sat by the wayside as Dad remedied the situation. Because of the delay and the slow mountain traveling, we arrived at our home long after midnight, exactly seven weeks from the day we left. Since no one knew we were coming, the house was both dark and cold. Even a roaring fire in both stoves made little impact on the frigid walls and woodwork. We staggered wearily to bed.

When we went back to school we were the envy of our classmates and the exasperation of our teachers. Of the four who were in school that year, two failed. The other two made it to the next grade only because their teachers were kinder. Dad and Mother did not seem to be concerned. After all, Dad had been taken out of school in the fourth grade, and Mother only went a grade or so farther.

Chapter 12

WET WHEELS

I shall never forget the day Dad had his first heart attack. He was working in the feed mill when the sharp pains struck him. He staggered to the house and sat in a chair. Mother, much alarmed, sent for the doctor in Canal Fulton, a town about five miles away.

When the doctor came he examined Dad and gave him medication which brought relief. Dad slowly recovered from that seizure, but sometime later was again stricken in the night. The pain was intense, and Dad thought he was dying. Not willing for his life to end, he prayed for healing so that he could rear his young family. The pain got worse. In greatest agony of body and spirit, Dad finally told the Lord he was willing to die if that was what He willed.

As the pain became even more intense, Dad began to praise the Lord he expected to see face to face in a few moments. Mother was praying and crying.

Suddenly the terrible pains ceased. Dad was still praising God, at first not aware that he had been healed! Before many days he was back to work again. In later years Dad had slight chest pains from time to time, but never again on the same scale as his first two attacks. He watched his diet carefully and was able to work hard for many years after the night he thought he was going home to Glory.

When we first attended the Sippo Church, it had two out-side entrances—one for men and one for women. Since the doors were not marked, visitors would sometimes wander in at the wrong door to the great amusement of us children. When they did this, the only way to get to the correct side (except for crossing in front of the first pew) was to go back outside and come in the other door.

The reason people couldn't rectify their mistake once they were inside was because a partition had been built into the center of the church. This barricade extended from the floor to the top level of the pews. It was very effective in keeping the men and boys on the right side and the women and girls on the left side.

The first time I heard the sheep and goats parable referred to in the Bible I immediately concluded that the men and boys were sheep, and women and girls were the goats. But Dad quickly debunked that chauvinist thinking by pointing out that from his place in the pulpit the distaff people were on the right side.

Dad was opposed to that dividing partition. He was also tired of the much too low and narrow benches which caused him to ache long before a service was over. So he proposed at one of the annual congregational councils that the partition be removed, the pews raised, and the seats widened. After the proposal was batted around negatively for a while, Dad sensed that it was going to be benched. He therefore offered to do all the work himself. And with that, the proposition was approved.

By the ingenious method of offering to do things himself, Dad was able to bring about a number of changes at the Sippo Church. The rigidly fastened pulpit which extended from one end of the platform to the other was reduced to a much smaller, movable one. The hissing gas lights (much like the Coleman lamps used today) were replaced with electric fixtures.

Dad also offered to redecorate the church, painting the woodwork and papering the walls and ceiling. This was a big undertaking, but was finally accomplished with the help of three very unenthused lads.

He got into serious trouble, however, on another improvement venture. The Sippo Church had no indoor plumbing, just two outdoor toilets. These small privies had no protecting walls to provide a sight barrier to an open toilet door. One day Dad decided to remedy this immodest situation without checking with the congregation. He supposed that everyone at church would pronounce blessings on him for his thoughtfulness and industry.

He purchased new lumber and built the screens which the law, even then, called for in public restrooms. On Sunday he waited for the plaudits of the people. To his amazement the money-minded members first asked what the cost was going to be. When assured that both labor and materials were *gratis,* they then wondered by whose authority he had cast out the evil situation. Since Dad had to admit going ahead on his own, the displeasure of all too many brothers and sisters was given center stage.

One brother who liked to wield power to make up for his lack of common sense suggested that the walls be torn down. Fortunately, wiser heads prevailed. Yes, Dad should be scolded for proceeding without proper clearances, but the walls would stay because they were needed.

We boys were indignant and thirsting for revenge. When we arrived at home, we had a plan. "Let's go right over to church tomorrow morning, Dad, and tear those walls down. Then all those mean people will be sorry for the way they treated you today!" But Dad shook his head, smiling sadly.

"Just remember the lesson you learned today, boys," he advised. "You can't even improve an outdoor toilet at the church without a ballot vote at the annual congregational council." In all the years I attended the Sippo Church after that incident, I never saw the offending walls without remembering the hubbub and Dad's wry comment.

The Brethren in Christ Church has practiced trine-immersion baptism from its inception. The *modus operandi,* probably borrowed from the German Baptist Brethren (Church of the Brethren), is to have the applicant kneel in water about thirty inches deep. The minister then administers baptism by having the person bow forward until completely under water. This is done three times, in the name of the Father, and the Son, and the Holy Spirit.

The Sippo Church had no baptistry, making it necessary to have baptismal services in a stream a mile away. This was always done after a Sunday morning worship service in the summer months. What an exciting day it was for children! What a day of blessing and rejoicing it was for believers, both those observing and those being baptized.

With everyone assembled at the water's edge, song books were handed out. The first song was always, "Shall We Gather at the River?" The congregation overlooked the obvious fact that the hymn speaks of end times when the saints will all be gathered together "at the throne of God."

When I pointed this out to the song leader one day, he just smiled. "Is that so? We will have to do something about that." I went home with elevated ego. At the next baptism service I

70

expected him to announce another hymn. But it was not to be, then, or ever. "Shall We Gather at the River?" continued to inspire the saints beside the stream as long as I attended Sippo baptisms.

Two baptism occasions stand out in bold relief. The first was the day I was baptized. Dad hoped to baptize his own boys, but the head minister, Bishop Myers, felt that he should do it in keeping with church tradition. Dad quietly agreed. But I was so angry about Dad's request being denied that I possibly entered the water a dry sinner and came out a wet one. My brothers Lloyd and Eli Jr., also baptized that day, were more forgiving.

As we came up out of the water, Dad and Mother hugged us and cried. I was embarrassed with such emotional display, not only by my parents, but by other members of the fellowship. It felt good, however, to feel the blest "tie that binds our hearts in Christian love." We were then whisked away to the Mohler home nearby for the change into dry clothes. And thus ended the final rite of our initiation into church membership.

Another baptism service also stands out clearly, but for an entirely different reason. Because of the distance from the road, families drove their cars through a broad meadow to the creek (always pronounced "crick"). On this Sunday the baptism service was ended and most people had already left. When our family piled into our car, the motor would not respond to the starter. So Dad resorted to the old faithful crank. Somehow he must have pulled the gear shift into low gear as he got out of the car.

As if the devil was in the engine, it caught hold on the very first pull. In that moment the car lurched forward, almost running over Dad. He somehow managed to sprawl over the hood and fender. Mother, who had not yet learned to drive, didn't know how to stop the car.

We were heading right for the creek. The car was in low gear, but that creek seemed to be getting closer awfully fast! Dad sort of rolled off the fender and onto his feet. He then jumped on the running board as the car came past and grabbed the steering wheel through the open window. No stuntman could have improved what happened next. With frantic effort, he pulled the wheel hard-left. The old Whippet responded, turning at the last possible moment to prevent its being baptized along with all the saints who had gone before!

71

Dad then reached far across and turned off the ignition key. We all jumped out to see how close we had come to going into the water. The track made by the right front tire was plainly evident, just inches from the edge of the bank which itself had almost caved in with the weight of the vehicle.

Although the creek was shallow, with little threat to life or limb, Dad prayed a prayer of praise to God for deliverance. The musical sound of the flowing water and the chirping and buzzing of the birds and insects made it a magical moment. We didn't sing "Shall We Gather at the River?" but we *were* "standing by the throne of God."

Dad had a deep hunger to bring about the conversion of his own people, the Old Order Amish. He felt that one way to accomplish this was to hold street meetings in their territory. Since no one else at our church was willing for such public exposure at first, the members of our family were elected.

Dad purchased a public address system which could be operated from a car battery. On a given warm evening we drove to one of the Amish towns and set up on the main corner. The program included testimonies, songs, and the message by Dad. Very few people were ever in sight, but the blast of the loudspeakers must have penetrated all but the thickest walls.

As a boy, I was a reluctant street evangelist, but didn't seem to have much choice. What Dad did, his family did. However, when he decided to herald the message loud and clear in our hometown, North Lawrence, my reluctance turned into stout resistance. Making a spectacle of myself in a strange village was one thing; doing so in front of my classmates was intolerable.

But Dad was determined. When the appointed night came, there we stood before our home community. It was sheer agony. I prayed that I would faint and be rushed off to the hospital. I hoped a drunk would stagger out of the saloon across the street and break up our meeting. But no such luck. Dad thundered while I suffered.

The next time Dad talked of a street meeting in North Lawrence, I tearfully begged to be relieved. When he saw how desperate I was, he relented. Very few decisions of his were ever more thankfully received.

Another way Dad felt would bring response from his Amish people was to hold evangelistic meetings in a large tent in their community. Although they lived twenty-five miles from the Sippo Church, his urging resulted in the Sippo Congregation venturing into Amish territory at least four times in the mid-thirties.

The large tent was twice pitched in the Mount Hope school yard. Rev. Henry Musser, a Pennsylvania Dutch preacher from Lancaster, Pennsylvania, was asked to preach for two reasons. First, he had a full beard and his haircut and clothes were very much like the Amish; and second, he could preach in German. When he visited among the Amish, he put them at ease by conversing in their native dialect. Then, a number of evenings during the meetings at carefully publicized times, he preached the whole sermon in German.

Dad was thrilled when the Amish attended the first night of the Mount Hope meetings rather well. His spirits remained high as they came back night after night. But as the days went by and none of them came forward at invitation time to pray (a few other people did respond), he began to get concerned.

The final night came. The tent was packed. The time for gathering in the net was at hand. Henry Musser exhorted in fine style, pacing back and forth on the plank platform and pounding the unvarnished pulpit. He then wound up the evening with an altar call which should have melted a heart of stone.

But not one Amish person responded.

Dad was cut to the heart. He, like Paul, would have been willing to be accursed if it could have helped bring the full assurance of eternal salvation to his own dear people. He searched his own life to see if he might have been a hindrance in the meeting. In the days following he fasted and prayed and wept. And he started talking about another tent meeting the next year.

The following summer the tent was again set up in the same school yard. Again, the good people of the Sippo Church pounded those weary miles night after night, spending money for gasoline they could ill afford. And again the response from the Amish was zero.

What a trial this was for Dad. But he still wouldn't give up. The next year the tent was again pitched in Amish country, this time in the Jeff Davis Woods near Shanesville. The Free Methodists in the area joined forces with the Brethren in Christ who drove the thirty-five miles every night. In this third attempt the attendance was again encouraging, but people hitting the sawdust trail raised very little dust.

I was always scared of the place. The day we were setting up the large tent a local man happened by and told us how the woods got its name. Some years before Jeff Davis, a Shanesville resident, mysteriously disappeared. A few days later someone found him in the woods near the tent site, hanging by the neck. Murder? Suicide? It was never determined.

Our informer lowered his voice, knowing full well he was scaring us younger listeners. "You know something," he whispered hoarsely, "the people on yonder farm say this place is haunted. Some nights they hear blood-curdling screams coming from these woods."

I could feel the hair bristle on the back of my neck, and looked to Dad for reassurance. He smiled, a bit weakly it seemed. "We trust in God, and our God has power over any evil spirit who ever lived."

"Hope you're right," drawled our friend, "but if I were you, I wouldn't stay around here late at night!" He started to walk away, but turned back. "See the big branch on that tree? That's where they cut old Jeff down." He looked at me and winked. "Don't worry, buddy. I think your daddy is right."

I *knew* my daddy was right, but was greatly relieved when the meetings ended without any screams in the night.

To my dismay the Sippo Congregation erected the tent in the Jeff Davis Woods the following summer. I had the same creepy feeling about the place. The people again stayed away from the mourner's bench in droves.

I really don't know if Dad was ready to give up on trying to evangelize the Amish after four annual efforts with such little success. But I do know that the Sippo people decided to invest their time and money in more fruitful areas. And Dad reluctantly agreed, it seems.

This is verified by the fact that even when he sponsored tent meetings himself in later years, he did not again attempt a direct ministry to the Amish. And still later, when he began mission work, he went to the city of Massillon, far from his beloved people. But he grieved for them all his days.

Chapter 13

PACKARD WHEELS

During the hilltop years Dad was involved in two additional jobs to keep the bill collectors satisfied. He still owned the muck farm a few miles away, working the land and keeping a few cattle. One winter he had around fifteen head of steers and they seemed to be doing well until one got sick and died. "That dead steer," moaned Dad, "represents all the profit I would have made."

His other venture was into the Rawleigh product business. The day his shipment of extracts, soaps, and what not came, our excitement was high as the colorful items were pulled out of the cartons. Then came the time to get out on the road and do a sales job.

When he came home after his first day as a Rawleigh man, Dad was rather subdued. Mother asked him how he had done, and he replied rather lamely that the sales were not too bad for the first day. But the second and following days were not much better.

One day Dad took me along. He was again having a run of bad luck; none of the housewives were buying. As he was getting out of the car to knock on another door, he looked at me in dejection and ventured, "Well, I'll go to the door now and make a liar out of another woman." I laughed, but I felt like crying. It really hurts, you know, to see your own father suffer as a failure.

The day wore endlessly on. When he came to one house which looked especially foreboding, Dad suggested that I take the basket loaded with all the goodies no one seemed to want and try my luck. "Go on, Paul," he coaxed. "If you make a sale, I'll give you half the profit." After more verbal arm-twisting, I went my way to the front door and knocked, hoping no one was at home.

But alas, footsteps soon sounded, and the door opened. I timidly proffered my wares, but the good housewife was distressed. "My God, how can a small boy like you be selling Rawleigh products?" I just hung my head. "Wait a minute, sonny," she said kindly. When she came back she pressed a nickel into my hand, squeezed my arm, and sent me on my way. I went down the path hating my heavy load of products, but loving that good woman with all my heart.

Dad was too discouraged to knock on any more doors, and I flatly refused, so we went home. Not many days later he decided that selling Rawleigh wares was not his calling. For years afterward, our household had an ample supply of vanilla extract and all its cousins. Whenever there was a shower for someone, our family could always be counted on for a good supply of spices, soaps, tooth brushes, and the like.

Making playthings for his family was much more interesting for both Dad and his children. One day he taught us how to make wooden guns that shot paper wads "faster than a speeding bullet," or almost so. First we went out to a Peter Tumbledown fenceline and found large elderberry stalks. We cut straight pieces an inch in diameter and about fifteen inches long. After we forced the soft pith out of the center, we had a hollow tube with the bore of a buffalo gun.

He next showed us how to make a ramrod out of an old steel rod from our junk pile by bending the rod at a point about an inch shorter than the elderberry tube. He then wrapped rags around the handle part, and we were ready for action.

Dad made a very large paper wad, about 60 caliber, chewing it until it was moist but not soggy. This was pushed into the near end of the gun which had been whittled funnel shaped, and rammed to the far end with the plunger. Then he made another wad and pushed it about an inch into the near end.

The big moment was at hand. The reputation of the elderberry gunsmith was at stake. Three boys stood by grinning with expectancy. Dad put the handle end of the plunger against his chest, placed the other end against the rear wad, gripped the muzzle firmly with both hands, and aimed the young cannon toward a neutral zone.

When he rammed the plunger home, the tight wad squeezed the air space between it and the front wad into a mighty small dimension in a mighty short time. With a bang worthy of a 12-guage shotgun, the front wad exploded from the muzzle and whammed into the far wall. What a blast!

Dad smiled. "Isn't that the berries?"

You elderberry gun experts will, of course, know that the gun was already loaded with a front wad for the next shot. When the day ended, my brothers and I went to bed with sore chests and aching jaws. But we had learned some interesting laws of physics without ever cracking a book.

For the first six years we lived in the area, our post office was named Bowdil. The village is in Lawrence Township. The township was named for the Lawrences who were among its earliest settlers. The only village in the township was in the northern section, so a very original soul named it North Lawrence.

How did the name get changed to Bowdil? Some years before we moved into the community two enterprising businessmen named Bowman and Dillon joined forces to build a factory beside the Pennsylvania Railroad which ran through the town. At their instigation, the appreciative townsmen agreed to rename the village Bowdil. They envisioned Bowdil becoming another Cleveland, or at least an Akron. But like the foolish man in the Bible, Bowman and Dillon failed to count the cost and ran out of money soon after the steel for the factory was in place.

Many times as we drove past the rustling skeleton, Dad would tell of their folly, mentioning the similar story in the scriptures. To the villagers, the structure was an eyesore. Bowman still lived in town, but Dillon (not Matt) had moved west. Someone circulated a petition to get the name changed back to North Lawrence.

Dad and I were busy working in the hatchery at the hilltop place when a man walked in, petition in hand. He carefully explained the whole problem to Dad and asked him to sign the paper. But Dad refused, and here is the reason he gave. "I have enough trouble spelling Bowdil (He sometimes spelled it Bowdel.), let alone a name as long as North Lawrence." He said this sincerely because he was a notoriously poor speller.

The petitioner argued his cause until his face became very red. When he finally realized that his elevated blood pressure was unavailing, he snatched up his paper and stomped out the door. All was quiet for a moment. Dad looked at me in amusement. "I don't think that man is in a mood to pray," he observed.

The red-faced Lawrencian must have been more successful with other township residents. In due time the town was reinstated to its former glory and named North Lawrence. "As it was in the beginning, is now, and ever shall be. . ." Dad

77

even learned to spell it correctly—most of the time.

One day in 1936 Dad drove a really different car home. Of all the automobiles he ever owned, that 1928 Packard was the best! It was a beautiful limousine which, in its day, was equal to the fanciest Cadillac or Lincoln Zephyr. It had luxurious grey upholstery and ingenious extra seats which folded into the back of the front seat.

The first Sunday we drove it to church the car created a sensation. And that is an understatement! We were the envy of all the children along with quite a few of their parents, no doubt.

One pious sister said, "Who does that Eli Hostetler think he is, anyhow?"

She was the same one who declared some years later when I spun my wheels on the gravel stones of the church parking lot, "I don't see how anyone can be saved and sanctified and spin his wheels!" When I heard it, I spun my wheels all the more. Dad observed that my carnal nature was showing. Whatever it was, spinning my wheels sure made me feel good.

Getting back to the Packard, the deacon at the church, a very mild mannered and charitable brother, opined that Dad was probably too poor to afford a huge straight-eight cylinder car that went de-quart, de-quart, de-quart even when it was idling.

The Packard was a dream car. It had hydraulic brakes and a built-in pressure system to pump up flat tires right out on the road. It had a heater that worked and a horn that made a beautiful two-note sound far superior to our Model-A Ford's rather hickish A-ooo-gah.

It is hard to believe, but in 1937 the State of Ohio had no age restriction on people having a driver's license. None at all. So, with Dad's blessing, backed by Mother's worrying, I took my test at the state police station and passed. Twelve years old and driving a car—some people had to be a little daffy, including the State, the police, and Dad.

As if that wasn't bad enough, Lloyd, eleven, also was issued a driver's license. One day Dad asked Lloyd to take the Packard to the welding shop in Massillon to get something repaired. With two cushions under him and about three behind, he headed for the city, looking through the space under the top of the steering wheel and above the instrument panel.

When he turned off the street and aimed that long hood toward the open door of the welding shop, the owner saw the Packard coming.

He took one look at what seemed to be a driverless car and ran for his life! How he enjoyed telling the story. "By golly," he would declare, "I was sure that Packard was out to get me!"

The big automobile could pass anything on the road except the filling stations, and that was its Achilles heel. Dad couldn't afford to feed the gas-guzzler. One sad day he drove it away, and with it went our abortive attempt at high society living.

Dad stayed with Fords from that time on. We children were vocal on the excellencies of Henry's cars and extolled their qualities with the undying determination peculiar to the uninformed. We argued with our peers and sometimes even took on an adult, generating much heat and little light. Dad, who was better acquainted with the foibles of Fords, would tell us sternly, "Stop arguing, or I'll buy a Chevy."

Despite the twinkle in his eyes, his threat was potent. Driving a Chevrolet to church would have been the epitome of shame for boys who staked their sacred honor on Fords.

Chapter 14

GRINDSTONE WHEELS

The Packard interlude did not get much retrospective attention because Dad was always making or changing something during the hilltop years. As the family grew larger in both size and number, more bedrooms were needed. Dad decided to build a second story above the ell which he had built on the original house moved from the farm. But, if he did that, the second floor would cut off the windows in the schoolhouse.

His recourse was to move the house, ell and all, south about ten feet. Dad accomplished this with the help of powerful jacks and the strong back of my uncle, Clarence Troyer. After building a new foundation, the two men went into action while life in the house went on as usual except that water pipes were shut off.

They eventually achieved their goal, but not without some frustrations. At one point a number of things went wrong in succession. Uncle Clarence in exasperation exclaimed, "Everything is going hay-wire!" Dad thought that was funny, and laughed heartily and long. Uncle Clarence soon became infected with Dad's good humor and joined him in laughter.

They then tackled the job with renewed strength and moved the house to the new foundation. The vacated space was filled with a new entrance hall, and a large bedroom was built for us boys right above the living room.

Dad hired a local plumber to help him put the large pipes in place which came down from the upstairs bathroom. The plumber, a big, friendly man, had only one besetting sin—he chewed tobacco almost constantly. Dad talked to him about his habit, both seriously and lightly. He liked to tell of the tobacco chewer who dropped his cud of tobacco while he was cleaning his henhouse. "And five different times he was sure he had found it (and here Dad would pause) until he put it into his mouth!"

Tobacco Chewer was big, but not overweight. Dad stood only five foot seven, but he weighed almost 200 pounds. Chewer, claiming his habit kept him from getting overweight, suggested that Dad take up the habit to get his weight down.

One day Chewer and Dad worked very hard in a rather small crawl space under the house (no basement) and finally had all the heavy pipes propped in place, ready to pour hot lead into the joints to seal them. But the pipes suddenly collapsed, causing a lot of elbow grease to go down the drain.

Dad looked at Chewer, and Chewer looked at Dad. "You know, Eli," he said as he unloaded a big squirt of tobacco juice, "you hang onto your religion, and I'll keep my mouth full of tobacco, and neither one of us will do any cussing!" They then put the pipes up to stay.

Our Jiffy-Dump truck gave us many miles of good service, but the little Model-T engine finally wore out. Dad studied the steel truck bed and decided to make a trailer. In due time he had a good trailer, but it had one serious drawback. It was so heavy that our car didn't have enough braking power to stop the trailer empty, let alone loaded.

After giving the problem quite a bit of consideration, Dad put together a device which automatically applied the brakes on the trailer wheels every time it thrust forward against the trailer hitch. It was a clever invention and should have been patented.

Thirty years later I rented a heavy trailer. When the agent hooked it up for me I noticed a device on the trailer tongue which looked hauntingly familiar. With beating heart I asked him what it was. He explained that it was an automatic brake and painstakingly showed how it worked.

Suddenly I was a boy back in Ohio again, watching and helping Dad with eager admiration. I assume someone came upon the same necessity Dad encountered and mothered the invention of the automatic brake. If only Dad had secured a patent on his idea and prototype, he might have amassed a fortune.

Dad was also far ahead of his day in dreaming of an automatic transmission for cars. He claimed that someone would someday use the principle Henry Ford had used in the transmissions of his Model-T's and make a fully automatic transmission. And one day someone did.

My brother Lloyd and Dad used to discuss the principle of

jet propulsion for airplanes long before it was used to power them. They called their brain-child an air-jammer. The idea was to take in cold air at the front of the air-jammer and heat it up as fast as possible. The resulting expansion would make a mighty blast out the back, pushing the airplane along.

Coming to a less lofty invention, Dad rigged up a camping trailer from scratch, and it worked beautifully. People looked at it in wonder, but that was all. A tent was made to be pitched on the ground, not on wheels. When in later years the pop-up trailer demand developed into a large industry, I often thought of what might have been, but by that time Dad had long since gotten rid of the trailer and was busy making something else.

He was always willing to have his children "help" him with his projects. One day, when my sisters Lois and Vange were still little tykes, Dad was painting furniture. When they begged for paint brushes, he got them each one.

The result, as Dad well knew it would be, was chaos. Some of the paint ended up on the furniture, but mostly it landed in other places. Lois says that "we slopped it all over!" About the only positive work that was accomplished that day was the building of a fond memory in two little lasses' hearts.

Lois and Vange learned how to "earn" money in early life. When kindly old Mr. Hess brought his usual few bags of grain to the mill to be ground, they put nails under his tires (while he was watching). The first time this happened he made the mistake of offering them a penny to take the nails away. They gleefully removed the nails and received their pay.

The next time Mr. Hess came the same ritual was repeated. Fortunately, the girls were otherwise occupied in most subsequent visits or else they would have depleted Mr. Hess' resources.

The little misses also made a game of pestering Dad when he was reading the newspaper. They hit the paper with a yardstick and pulled on his arms. Dad would complain, "For pity sakes! Why is it my ill fate to have two such troublesome daughters?"

We had an old grindstone made out of sandstone about two feet in diameter. When Dad sharpened knives or chisels he sat on the seat and worked the pedals to make the stone spin. One day George, just a little duffer, became interested.

He pushed a box over to the grindstone, climbed up on it,

and leaned in close to the place where the knife and stone were rubbing together. In fact, he got so close that his nose pushed against the spinning stone! Result—a skinned and slightly sharpened nose.

"Now that," exclaimed Dad, "is keeping your nose to the grindstone!"

Chapter 15

ELEVATOR WHEELS

As mentioned before, one of the many businesses Dad was engaged in on the hill was raising broilers for market. The chicks were started in small battery brooders and, as a new batch was hatched in the incubators each week, the older ones were moved on to ever larger brooders. All the smaller brooders were commercially made, but the larger ones were designed and built by Dad.

Hundreds of the smaller brooders stood in long rows and at different levels. The broilers lived in apartments, as it were. Each separate pen had a flat pan under it to catch the droppings. And those pans were always getting loaded. And what is far worse, Dad's boys had the chore of unloading them.

The small brooders were on the second floor of the schoolhouse. Dad cut a hole in the floor, put a chute under the hole, and had a very large hand cart at the lower end. Three times a week we boys had to pull the pans from under each pen, trudge over to the hole, and scrape off the offensive smelling droppings with a small shovel. We hated the job with a passion.

One day Eli Jr. and I were assigned to pull and tote and scrape. The day was hot and our tempers raw. Eli made an insulting remark, and I became so incensed that I flung the shovel at him. My aim was poor and Eli was about twenty feet away and heading east fast. No kidding, he really was heading east. The shovel nicked him on the arm as it went whizzing past. Eli grabbed his appendage and let out with a scream intended to bring parental action. It did.

Dad came running up from the feed mill as Eli continued his loud moans. After all the evidence was weighed, the verdict was: Paul shall finish cleaning off all the dropping pans while Eli is excused to recover from his hurt. Since we had barely started with the cleaning job that day, I was madder than ever. But Dad made his ruling stick; throwing a shovel, after all, could inflict severe damage.

What was really galling, Eli later admitted to me that he hadn't really been hurt at all. "But I didn't mind the good rest," he grinned. I almost hit him again.

The brooders on the main floor, right under the others, were Dad's creations. The main difference, aside from the pens being larger, was that the droppings were handled in a different way. A long roll of paper was started at one end of a long section of pens and pulled under the cages all the way to the other end. A large wooden roller was mounted at the brooder's end and the paper fastened to it. Each roller had a crank and steel scraping blade. Now, the *theory* was top rate, but carrying it out was otherwise.

The big, almost ready for market broilers really loaded the paper, and the moisture from the droppings soaked in. Often when we turned the crank the paper tore. When that happened the only thing left to do was to grab the paper (and manure) in our hands, one boy on each side, and gently move it along.

Dad remedied the situation by getting paper which had more tar along with other reinforcements. Although it never tore, it wrinkled so bad that a prune would be considered smooth as a fresh plum by contrast. The wrinkles rubbed up against the wire mesh that held the broilers, and really gummed up the works.

Furthermore, the blade at the end just wouldn't scrape much of the droppings off. It was awful. We never did find a paper that worked right. If only it had been a later day, rolls of modern plastic would have made Dad's contrivance sheer wizardry.

When enjoying delicious fried chicken today, I eat with thanksgiving to the unfortunate persons who do all the dirty work connected with getting the fowl to my plate. And I aid my digestion by meditating on dropping pans and related matters.

After we had lived on the hill for a while, running the feedmill and cider press, and hatching chicks and raising broilers, even more income was needed. Dad therefore decided to develop a henhouse in the schoolhouse attic. To get us up there, he bought and installed a used, hand-operated elevator. Pulling the endless rope which hauled us to the top was hard work, but the trips down were fun. We let 'er fly all the way, pulling the brake lever at the last possible moment.

The hens did fairly well in the attic, but the place was infested with rats. Dad offered us five cents for every rat we killed, so we got traps for places inaccessible to the hens and also shot the pests with our rifle.

One night one of us fired the rifle at a rat which ran into the eaves of the schoolhouse on the side near our house. The bullet missed the rat (as usual), went through a soft pine board, jumped the ten-foot gap between school and house, plowed through the soft siding and the plasterboard inside, and lodged in the headboard of a bed in our bedroom.

When we went to bed that night, I found the bullet there. We took a jack knife and pried out the missile, but didn't tell Dad until much later. We *did,* however, aim in other directions when shooting rats.

Dad admonished us to always be careful when using the rifle. Again and again he showed us the words of warning on the boxes of cartridges: "Caution—dangerous within one mile!" But we sometimes forgot.

One day we were knocking tin cans off a post with the gun. After many shots, Eli Jr. noticed that we were pumping bullet after bullet into the roof of our neighbor's house about eighty yards away. We immediately hied around the end of the chickenhouse and suffered through the evening and the next days, waiting for the telephone call or visit from an irate neighbor. It never came.

Perhaps our deadly accuracy in hitting the can almost every time caused the slugs to veer. And then, perhaps the bullets slamming into a roof from a low trajectory didn't cause leaks. The mystery remains unsolved.

One more rifle story. We always kept the rifle, not loaded, on brackets in the entrance hall. Dad protested mildly. The cartridges were stored in a cabinet nearby.

One Halloween night a couple of kids from North Lawrence boldly soaped our living room windows while we were sitting there. I raced across the room and into the hall, snatched the rifle and some shells, and loaded the gun as I rushed out the door. By that time the two boys were already out on the road and heading for home. I shouted, "Stop, or I'll shoot!" But the boys kept on going.

Just as Dad came out of the house I squeezed off a shot, high enough over their heads to be totally safe, yet low enough so that they would hear the whine of the bullet. The boys were running before, but they kicked up a lot more dust after. Dad objected to the shooting but obviously enjoyed seeing the boys hightail it toward town.

The next day at school the word was going around that Preacher Hostetler had fired three shots at two boys who hadn't been doing anything bad at all, and that the shots whizzed by only inches over their heads. When I learned that the boys involved were the school bullies, I was especially delighted. I never corrected their story—and they never beat me up after the shooting.

Dad relished telling stories. He was frequently in fine fettle at our family dinner table. When there was work to be done, we children were adept at getting him to relate our favorite stories over and over again. We thought we were manipulating him to our advantage but later learned that he was aware of our scheme all along.

One of our most often asked-for tales involved Dad and his brother Sol. Sol was clever in addition to being strong, and Dad suffered at his hands more than once.

One day Sol asked if he was interested in a game of mumbly-peg. In this game they used a pocket knife with two blades. One blade was opened full out while the other, hinged at the same end, was positioned perpendicular to the handle and other blade.

The players faced each other with a board or plank between. The object was to flip the knife into the air in such a way that it would stick into the wood when it landed. Their wooden porch floor worked very well, but Mother was prone to clear the deck with a broomstick. Grandma Hostetler was no hockey player, but she was a good stick-handler and capable of a stinging slap-shot!

Sol and Dad agreed to play in the barn. They hauled out a large plank and balanced it across a crate near the horse stable. As the game progressed, with Dad scoring much better than Sol for a change, he became so engrossed with his good fortunes that he failed to notice his end of the plank being slowly maneuvered toward the back of the horse stall.

Just as Dad was sure he was winning, Sol jumped off the plank, and the grinning mumbly-peg winner was suddenly dumped into the horse manure. Sol went charging out of the barn yelling his glee and turning handsprings to the consternation of clucking hens and quacking ducks.

As for Dad, he picked himself up, brushed off the foul-smelling stuff as much as possible, and headed for the house for a change of clothes. He later "got even," but not in the way Sol expected.

Dad had an inventive mind, even in his youth. One day he made an "engine" by taking a long rope and putting it through a pulley high up on the wall of the barn. He then put a heavy weight on one end and a wooden axle about two inches in diameter at the other end. He rigged up his invention so that when he moved a lever his engine ran, pulled by the weight. He carefully concealed rope and weight and pulley.

He then called in Sol who, after taking one look, stated flatly that Eli couldn't make an engine which would run. He watched scornfully as Dad walked over and pulled the "throttle." How Dad enjoyed watching Sol's eyes bulge as the engine hummed with power!

After starting and stopping his motor a number of times, Dad shut it off for the final time—just before the weight reached the bottom. Sol called for more action, but Dad refused. Suspicious, he looked around for a tool to tear the engine apart. But Dad had anticipated this and hid all the tools.

Sol ranted and raged, claiming the engine was a fake, but Dad held firm. As far as he was concerned, the horse manure account was settled.

Dad made a more practical piece of machinery not long after. He carefully studied the huge threshing machine a neighbor operated and then made a miniature one of his own. What is more, it worked. When he persuaded a willing worker to rapidly turn the crank, the tiny cylinder whirled while all the other shaking and spinning parts did their thing. Sol just shook his head in wonder.

The pig story was high on our list of favorites. The fences on the Henry Hostetler farm had weak spots, and the pigs were intent on finding them. One day an especially cantankerous old sow went through the fence, and Dad was given the job of getting her back. He first located the hole in the fence and then chased the sow back to the opening. But she didn't seem able to see it, going past time after time.

When Dad told Sol of his frustrations, Sol promised to "really fix that old hog." He got the family 12-guage shotgun off the rack. He next took a shell and emptied out the pellets, replacing them with coarse salt. After loading the gun, he got into position near the hole in the fence and asked Dad to bring on the ornery critter.

Just as the weak-eyed beast was opposite the hole, the shotgun BANGED. The sow gave a shrill squeal and went through the fence in a single bound—three feet away from the original hole!

Now the boys had two holes to mend, but they didn't mind. It *did* take quite a while because of recesses for additional fits of laughter. As for the sow, she learned her lesson well. She didn't break through the fence again for at least a week.

That narrative would generally bring on another shotgun story.

A man living in the Mount Hope vicinity was a notorious chicken thief, and had a special liking for the chickens at one particular farm. One night the farmer saw the thief enter his chicken house, bag in hand.

He quickly got his shotgun and took a roundabout route to the orchard through which the thief had come. Sure enough, after a while Chicken-Stealer came through the orchard with the stolen chickens in his bag. After Stealer passed, Farmer quietly followed him. When he got to the fence at the edge of the orchard, Stealer lifted the bag over and placed it on the ground. He then stooped to go through the fence himself.

BANG!

Stealer yelled and dove through the fence with six feet to spare on the other side! He picked himself up and headed for home in what was probably the first four-minute mile. Farmer picked up his bag of chickens and went back to calm the fears of his anxious wife.

Things were notably quiet on the chicken-stealing front after that night. Farmer wondered about the condition of Stealer's posterior. A few weeks later word filtered back from a doctor in another county that a man had come in "to have a saucer-full of shot removed from his behind." The patient explained that he had been involved in a hunting accident.

When Dad told this story, we boys always suggested that Sol should have been there to shoot salt into the wound to help it heal!

Chapter 16

WATER WHEELS

In my twelfth summer Dad and Mother were invited to assist Henry Schneider, a fiery Michigan preacher, in a new frontier of evangelism in Rust, Michigan. The small settlement, which presumes to call itself a village, is in the general vicinity of Alpena.

After the large tent had been set up, Dad's homemade house trailer parked under a friendly tree, and the cook tent and other needed sleeping tents pitched, Dad gave his attention to a more (to me) important matter—fishing.

We were told some hard to believe stories about the size of fish being caught in Fletcher Pond, the backwater of a large nearby dam. Money for casting rods was an out of reach luxury, so we borrowed long cane poles. The first morning we set forth before daybreak. It was raining and cold, and we came home wet and chilled. As Dad put it, we had "Fisherman's luck—no fish and empty gut."

A day or so later we tried again, and with more success. Fishing with minnows, we landed northern pike much larger than the bluegills we pulled out of Ohio streams. One day the big ones were biting. Just as it became necessary for us to head home in order to arrive in time for the evening tent meeting, a really big fish splashed out of the water about a hundred yards from the boat.

It surfaced again some seventy-five yards away. And again fifty yards from us. After the same time interval, it arched majestically about twenty-five yards away. We counted the seconds in the quiet of the summer evening. Then, just as Dad said, "He ought to be here right now," his bobber zipped under the water. He hauled up hard on the long pole and shouted, "I got him!"

The pike was not in agreement and swam away full speed. In moments the pole and line were stretched straight out from the boat. Fortunately, Dad had the presence of mind to let the pole fly. To my dismay, the pole headed away from us at top fish speed.

Dad yelled for me to get the anchor aboard and scrambled for the oars. He rowed over to the pole, now lying quietly in the water. I was sure that our big one had gotten away. But when we pulled on the line, the fish went into action with renewed determination. Since our boat was now free in the water, Dad kept the pole up and forced the churning Northern to pull us around. He pulled viciously, causing the line to hiss as it sliced the water. The boat spun around again and again, but Dad hung on.

Suddenly the line went limp. Dad quickly assured me that the pike was still hooked although he had given up the battle. Moments later we had him safely in the boat—all thirty-six inches of him. I was so excited I jumped up and down in the small boat and almost fell overboard. "Well praise the Lord," exclaimed Dad, "now we can go home."

We arrived back at the scene of the spiritual battle later than Pastor Schneider approved of. Dad should have known better but he couldn't resist holding up our big fish. The preacher was short and to the point. "Jesus called His disciples from that kind of fishing to a more important kind." And he pointed toward the large tent.

Dad quietly put our prize catch away and we cleaned up for the evening service. I felt bad about Pastor Schneider's remark until Dad said, "Don't let that bother you too much, Paul; Jesus served His disciples fish for breakfast *after* He called them to be fishers of men. He must have caught the fish Himself."

We went fishing on other days during the two-week series, but we always came home in good time before the evening service. We caught many more good fish, but none nearly as big as the one which made us late. I suggested to Dad that the whoppers bite only in the evening, but without success.

The Monday after the meetings closed, Dad convinced Henry Schneider to go fishing with us. When he hooked a small 14-inch pike, he immediately hauled it out of the water with his long pole. The pike swung across our boat and almost hit Dad, and then swung far out to the other side of the boat before returning for a pass at me.

We finally stopped the fishy pendulum. I was utterly disgusted with the preacher's fishing technique; if he had fished a bit more during the meetings, he would have known how to handle himself the day following.

Following the meeting, a small church was built in Rust. Fourteen years later I preached for an evangelistic series there. I again fished in Fletcher Pond, but without success. Far too many fishermen had been there in the intervening years, and besides, Dad wasn't there to show me how.

A summer or so later Dad was asked to fill in for four weeks at the Brethren in Christ Home Mission Board's church near Knifley, Kentucky. It was again my good fortune to be included as Dad and Mother briefly sojourned in those beautiful hills south of the Bluegrass Country.

We were located at the Home Evangel mission station on Robinson Ridge. It seems like all the topography in that part of Kentucky is either a ridge or a "holler." We arrived on a Saturday at the home of Albert Engle, the mission superintendent living near Columbia, and he took us over to the ridge the next day for the Sunday service.

My first exciting impression of Kentucky grew out of that trip. As we drove along through the scenic valley, we were suddenly confronted with a good sized stream with a bridge nowhere in sight. The gravel road simply went to the edge of the water, disappeared, and then showed up again at the far shore.

Superintendent Engle's procedure for crossing streams was interesting and, according to Dad, wrong. He crossed through the water slowly, all the while racing the car engine, slipping the clutch as he went. His method no doubt met its Waterloo when automatic transmissions came in.

We crossed the creek successfully and went dripping on our way. In less than a mile we encountered and crossed the same stream again. Another quarter mile, and the act was repeated! Dad wondered why the road builders didn't follow a slightly different route and eliminate two of the crossings. I thought three crossings were far better!

After a few more miles, we came to the end of the valley and the beginning of the climb to Robinson Ridge. The ruts and high points in the narrow road were a challenge to negotiate and devastating to the underparts of the car. Dad found it impossible to eliminate all the scrunching and crunching sounds as rocks and hardpan encountered muffler and oil pan.

We arrived at the Sunday afternoon meeting, being held in a small, frame schoolhouse, a few minutes late. The opening song was already being sung, and it composed my next positive impression of the Kentucky people. The singing was hearty, with the singers obviously enjoying it. The tempo was lively—the kind that impels even the most solemn elder to tap his foot.

The summer afternoon was hot and some worshippers were barefooted. Others were in denim overalls. I thought this was a great idea and did the same from that time on. One grandmother was sitting in a rocking chair outside the open door, creaking away in time to the music.

We learned to love those dear people for their honesty and hospitality. I liked the way they responded when Dad asked about their spiritual welfare.

"Are you a Christian?" he would ask.

"No sir, Preacher; I am just a plain, ordinary sinner," was the response often given.

That quality of frankness was new to me then, and I have seldom heard it since. How refreshing! One is reminded of the Pharisee and publican praying in the temple. The Pharisee proudly reminded God that he was not as other men were, especially the publican. The publican, like the good Kentucky people, simply admitted he was a sinner and in need of help.

Hospitality was another characteristic of the Kentucky folks. We were dinner guests in one home, and a huge platter of chicken was on the table surrounded with many other goodies. When the chicken was passed around, I took a medium sized piece as a starter. A few minutes later the hostess spied my piece, jumped to her feet, and rushed around the table.

She came upon me so quickly and protesting "No, no, NO!" that I cringed back, being sure some unforgivable sin had been committed. She snatched the piece of chicken off my plate and quickly carried it back to her own. She then ran to the platter, forked off the biggest piece in sight, and plunked it on my plate!

Now, there's no point in resisting such determination, especially when you don't feel like it. That piece of chicken was a forerunner of Colonel Sanders' golden delicacies. You see, it was deep-fried in southern love.

Kentucky farmers grew succulent watermelons, and our family loved to eat them. A nearby farmer was selling them out of his field, two for a quarter. One evening we stopped for two melons. The farmer brought two huge ones and then said,

"Wait a minute; I'll give you another one." When he came back with the third melon, it was larger by far than the two we paid for!

That night we sat around and ate watermelon until late. I was allowed to eat piece after piece. The problem with eating melons, to quote another, is that one's ears get so wet! But I discovered another problem. I awakened in the middle of the night with a wet sheet under me. Burning with shame, I called Mother. Such a thing had not happened since I quit wearing diapers some time after my first birthday.

Mother got me cleaned up and removed the damaging evidence from the bed. She made me a comfortable floor bed and returned to her own bedroom. It was a long time before I went back to sleep. Thankfully, Dad never mentioned the incident to me. Perhaps Mother didn't tell him. And I have eaten the sugary, red mini-blimps with real moderation ever since.

A boy who lived near the mission house could shoot a sling shot with deadly accuracy. When I asked him to improve my skills, he gladly assented. He showed me how to shoot by demonstrating his ability, but try as I would, my stones hardly ever hit the mark.

One day I was strolling around looking for suitable targets when I spied the dipper hanging on the water pump in the back lawn. Someone had ingeniously fashioned a gourd into a dipper which worked very well. The small end of the gourd was the handle, and the other end, about four inches in diameter, was the drinking cup.

Dad was sitting nearby, observing my frustrations without being too much comfort. "Practice makes perfect," he offered, not very originally.

When he saw me draw a bead on the gourd-dipper he said, "If you hit that gourd, you'll put a hole through it." But he didn't seem worried. I was, after all, standing fifty feet from the pump. So I let fly. All my previous practices were made perfect in that shot. The stone not only hit the gourd, it hit the bottom of the dipper dead center.

I can hear the pop of the dry shell yet and see the symmetry of the hole. I can also recall the look of pleased pain on Dad's face. He was happy that I had evolved into a modern David, but was pained with the Goliath I had slain.

I stood there with sling shot drooping. "I yi yi yi," said Dad. He examined the gourd and declared it unfixable. The next time we went to town he bought a new metal cup. Perhaps it would be more correctly said that *I* bought the cup because my hard-earned cash was used.

Later in the summer we moved to a valley called Spout Springs, so named because a spring of cold water gushed out of the hillside and made its final run in a steel spout. The mission superintendent was the evangelist for a tent meeting near the spring, and we lived in a couple of smaller sleeping and cooking tents.

One day Dad asked me if I had ever made water wheels and put them into a stream. He, of course, knew the answer since he had been around for most of my life. He found pine boards on a scrap-heap and opened his jack knife. He patiently whittled a super water wheel with his sharp blade.

The next job was to find a suitable place to install it. We walked along the stream which flowed near our tents for quite a distance before he settled on a location. I hadn't noticed, but the water there was running quite a bit faster due to the steeper drop and narrower shores.

Dad then moved some stones and rocks around to channel the water into an even narrower place. He made a trough out of three six-inch boards, nailing them together so that they looked like a flat-bottomed "U" when viewed from the end. The whole thing was about six feet long. Dad wedged this trough in place with rocks to keep it from washing away in the current.

The water came in at the upstream end of the trough six inches deep, but it was less than half that deep by the time it reached the downstream end. Having cut notches into the top edges of the trough for the nail-axles of the water wheel to turn in, he showed me that the water wheel turned only half as fast in the deep, upper end as it did in the shallow, lower end.

"Now, why do you think that is happening?" asked Dad. "You would think the wheel should run faster in the deepest water."

I studied the situation for a while, moving the wheel from one end to the other, and it always ran much faster at the downstream end. Suddenly the light came. "I have it!" I exclaimed. "In order for the water to be only half as deep at the lower end of the trough, it must be going twice as fast as the water at the upper end."

Dad's eyes sparkled with pride. "Paul, you have a head like a brass tack!" It was a wonderful moment, and the glow lingers. If only more dads would praise their children. If only I had done it oftener. I had good intentions, but I waited too long. To paraphrase Tevia in *Fiddler on the Roof,* I one day looked at my grown-up daughters and asked:

Are these the little girls I carried?
Are these my little ones at play?
I don't remember growing older,
When did they?
Wasn't it only yesterday when they were small?

Sunrise, sunset, swiftly fly the years,
One season following another,
Laden with happiness and tears.

Dad showed me how to make other kinds of water wheels and how to hook up two of them to moving objects: a funny man sawing wood and a chipper bird bobbing its tail up and down.

With room for additional water wheels, Dad suggested that I complete the project alone. After some days three more wheels were in the trough along with a teeter-totter and a cow swishing her tail. It was quite a menagerie, and they all moved at different speeds.

While we worked on the project, other children came by and watched in fascination. They then went upstream to construct their own water wheel complex. But, with no dad to give sure-handed guidance, the water in their trough moved sluggishly and their poorly constructed water wheel refused to run.

A few days before our stay in the serene valley was ended, my six water wheels and everything that pertained to them disappeared. Terribly upset, I walked at least a mile upstream and the same distance with the flow of the water looking for my lost treasures, but to no avail.

I came back and sat on the shore where I had often sat to watch the untiring creatures in action. The water flowed by endlessly and musically. The birds twittered and a cow bell sounded in the distance. But I cried bitterly as have countless others who have been the victims of those who violated God's Eighth Commandment.

I remembered the time about six years earlier when Dad came home from town with silver banks for each of his three eldest sons, with the promise that when they were filled he would take us to the bank to open a savings account for each one. Eli Jr., Lloyd, and I deprived ourselves of many pieces of candy and ice cream cones as the beautiful chrome banks slowly got heavier and heavier.

About the time it was becoming difficult to insert more coins, Dad hired a man who happened along, asking for work. He was a hard worker, and Dad was pleased with him. One night Dad and Mother went to a revival meeting with the whole family except George, who was the baby, and the hired man took good care of him.

Not many days later the hired hand vanished while the family was gone. Mother discovered that the money in her jar in the kitchen cupboard was gone. We next looked for our silver banks, and they were also missing. Dad went to the shed where his good tools were kept; some of them were also taken.

I shall never forget the feeling of loss we boys experienced. It was the darkest day of our life. Dad replaced the banks and encouraged us to fill them again, but we didn't respond. An ice cream cone in hand was far better than money in the bank.

The hired man who stole our banks broke a commandment, and the person who stole my water wheels broke the same commandment. God has forgiven them if they repented, but even at this late date I find it hard to forgive the thieves who pilfered my savings and made off with my hand-carved treasures.

Dad tried to comfort me as he had six years earlier. In fact, he offered to help me replace the stolen goods. But it was no use. I just didn't have the heart to start all over again.

A week later we headed back to Ohio and home. Our vacation in Kentucky was ended. And most of our memories were pleasant.

Chapter 17

CREATION WHEELS

The youngest child of the family was born on August 30, 1941. For the first time, Mother had very difficult and long labor. However, when it was all over, mother and son Virgil Lee were both doing fine.

Dad believed the Bible. Literally. And according to the Good Book the sun went around the earth each day. One day I came home from school with the proud knowledge of a seventh grader. That day the teacher had convinced me the earth went around the sun. He showed us, by holding a globe in his hand, how the four seasons of the year come about because the earth is tilted 23.5 degrees on its axis in relation to the sun, and that it travels around the sun once each year.

Then he explained that the earth is rotating on this axis every twenty-four hours, making it *seem* like the sun rises each morning and sets each night. This was mind-boggling to a lad who had heard Dad's version. So I went home to set Dad straight.

He listened quietly. Now, Dad had a mind which responded to reason, and the teacher's explanation all seemed reasonable to me even if it forced me to discard some rather firmly entrenched notions. So I thought he would admit his error.

But not so. He simply opened his Bible and read from Joshua 10:12-14.

Then spake Joshua to the Lord in the day when the Lord delivered up the Amorites before the children of Israel, Sun, stand thou still upon Gibeon; and thou, Moon, in the valley of Ajalon.

And the sun stood still, and the moon stayed, until the people had avenged themselves upon their enemies. Is not this written in the book of Jasher? So the sun stood still in the midst of heaven, and hasted not to go down about a whole day.

And there was no day like that before it or after it, that the Lord hearkened unto the voice of a man: for the Lord fought for Israel.

Then he closed his Bible and looked me squarely in the eyes. "Paul, I believe every word in the Bible, even when it contradicts what you learn in school. And I want you to believe every word in the Scriptures, even when they do not agree with what your teachers tell you."

When I told Dad I was not challenging the fact that God provided an unusually long day for Joshua when he prayed, he thought he had won the argument. But when I suggested that our powerful God could as easily stop the earth from spinning on its axis as stop the sun in its orbit, he totally rejected that line of reasoning.

"If you start to explain away this miracle exactly as it happened, Paul, you will soon explain away more important parts."

In the years since, I have learned the orthodoxy of Dad's statement. All too often when people nibble away at the accuracy of the Bible in what seem to be unimportant considerations, they also reject crucial doctrines such as Jesus being born of a virgin.

Dad never changed his mind on the sun going around the earth. It really bothered me at the time to have so naive a progenitor, but Dad went blithely on, having a much more wonderful time than many a person who was better informed in the follies of knowledge.

When I later confronted the theory of evolution in my tenth grade biology class, he was terribly upset. "It's just a theory, Dad," I pointed out. But to him even *thinking* about evolution was of the devil. The subject was so painful to him that I never brought it up again.

In due time when I learned that both the earth and man are much older than the 6,000 years Bishop Ussher allowed, Dad was emphatic in denying such a possibility. His mind was simply closed to such "ungodly nonsense." I, like Mark Twain, found my father exceedingly stupid in my early years, and it was a sore trial to me but, also like Twain, I was amazed at how much wiser he later became.

He also had very firm beliefs on how one should dress in

99

the wintertime in northern Ohio—with long underwear. A corollary to that was absolutely no shorts in physical education classes or, indeed, anywhere. This combination of rules caused me much embarrassment in high school.

The gym teacher was willing to go along with the no-shorts conviction, and he really didn't care about my long underwear either. However, the one-piece "Union Suit" put me into a real bind in another way. When we played basketball in gym class, one team was always asked to be "skins" by taking off their shirts. In this way players on the respective teams could easily be identified in the rush of the game. The other team were "shirts."

Since I was also forbidden to take a shower at school, I hid my distressing problem for quite a while by pleading for the team I was on to be shirts. But one day that failed, and I had to admit to the whole class that even if I took my shirt off I couldn't strip to the waist because of my long underwear. The coach, a rather loud and rough-spoken man, shrugged his shoulders. "So what?" he asked quietly; "Let Paul's side be the shirts." And that's the way it was until winter ended.

That solved the immediate problem, but I do feel that being forced to wear long underwear to high school put a psychological mark on me that stunted me for life. Or something like that.

More liberated parents laughed at Dad's quaint convictions, sure that he was out of touch and behind the times. And they were right—in some respects. In matters that really counted, however, he was in full touch with truth. One who is walking with God to the best of his ability is as up to date as tomorrow.

During our hilltop years, my two brothers and I became obsessed with the idea of having a squirrel. A friend of ours caught a fox squirrel in a box trap and kept it in a large cage. And so we had to have one too.

Dad was opposed to the idea. He said squirrels were meant to climb trees and gather nuts. But we boys built a box trap and set it out in the woods. On the third day we were successful, and our prey was a little red-squirrel.

Since Dad was not in favor of our project, we didn't ask him to help us make a cage for our cute little nutcracker. We worked long and hard, but the result was a disaster—a cage neither round nor square. The steel mesh was unyielding and sharp, causing bleeding fingers and blistered tempers.

Finally we went to Dad with downcast eyes and asked him to help us. He came to our "cage." "For pity sakes!" he declared in wonder, and his words said it well. But he soon got "that" look in his eyes, and we knew that a super cage was already beginning to take shape. Dad never worked from drawings; he just started cutting and putting together. He built us such a beautiful cage for little Reddie that our friend with the fox squirrel was left in the minor leagues.

It had a "tree" in it, made from a real tree. It had a little box for Reddie to sleep in, and the box looked just like a tiny house. One branch of the tree had a miniature wagon wheel mounted at an angle, and Reddie learned to run on it, spinning the wheel swiftly while he ran in one place. Beyond a doubt, Dad's finished product could have been named a nutcracker suite.

Dad warned us to feed Reddie only certain kinds of food such as nuts and grains. As far as we could tell, he was healthy and happy. One day when Dad and Mother were gone, we discovered that he liked jelly-bread. In fact, he loved it. Foolishly we gave him all he wanted. That night when Mother tried to feed him, he wouldn't eat. She wondered why, and we felt guilty.

The next morning Reddie was at the bottom of his cage— dead. When the story of disobedience came out, our parents were disappointed in us, but also deeply sympathetic. We children dug a little grave under a tree in our back yard and placed a little board there, simply inscribed, "Reddie."

I think of Reddie every time I drive through a nearby park filled with squirrels. One tree near a drive has a sign with these delightful words:

Please drive slowly.
Our squirrels don't know
One nut from another.

That was Reddie's problem too.

Chapter 18

TRAIN WHEELS

One time, after a season of prayer and fasting, Dad became burdened with the realization that he didn't really care enough about unsaved people. He therefore began to pray that God would give him a vision of what it meant for just one soul to be lost. I can remember him praying the prayer at our family altar.

What resulted as an answer to that prayer is firmly riveted to the strongest wall of my memory. God chose to answer Dad's plea and showed him the stark terror experienced by one person being eternally separated from God. It was, perhaps, the most dreadful experience Dad ever went through. He would walk around the house, the mill, and other buildings, wringing his hands and weeping in deepest agony.

This went on day after day as Dad was bereft of both food and sleep. The rest of our family were not doing very well either because this continued at all hours of the day and night.

Dad finally realized that he would have to get relief or die. He prayed that God would take away enough of the burden for him to resume necessary duties with his family. This God lovingly did. But the burden never totally left him and ultimately resulted in his selling out and going into mission work. Prayers can be rather costly at times.

The year I turned sixteen Dad decided to keep me out of school, as Ohio laws allowed. Having just completed my sophomore year in high school, I rebelled against quitting. But all my pleading fell on deaf ears. Dad needed me in the feedmill and cider press and chicken business. And so I put away my childish studies and became a man.

In looking back, it seems that Dad must have been watching me more closely than I could have suspected. As the days wore endlessly on, Dad one electric day said that if I put in a good year of work he would send me to Messiah College the next fall. Messiah College! A dream of dreams.

My mind went back to the day the Messiah College Male Chorus gave a program in the Sippo Church when I was a boy. Our little church was filled on a warm spring afternoon, with no place for the chorus of about thirty young men to sit. They therefore stood outside the church until the time came for them to sing.

When given the signal, they came marching down both aisles and stood three-deep across the front of the church. Professor Earl Miller called for the blowing of a pitch pipe, and the chorus quietly hummed in four parts. I was sitting with our family at our usual spot, second center pew from the front.

I expected something good, but was not prepared for the startling impact of thirty male voices joining in hearty harmony a bare six feet away. Sound in full third dimension and glorious technicolor swept all around us! The whole place throbbed with the heavenly vibrations of tenor, baritone, and bass.

Before the male chorus had completed their first selection, I had a dream. I would grow up, and go to Messiah College, and sing in that chorus. Any education was incidental. Singing in that chorus was the thing!

All of this and more surged through my mind that day in the mill as Dad sat on a bag of dairy supplement and I leaned against the feed mixer. I wanted to hug Dad but was far too shy. But I hugged him with my eyes. He surely must have known.

He went on to say he could plainly see I wasn't meant for the feedmill because my nose was always in a book (sometimes hidden among the feed sacks). And furthermore, he and Mother wanted their boys to be preachers, and Messiah College would surely help that cause along. I didn't have the heart to tell him I had other ideas. The possibility of going to Messiah College (which included a Christian high school then) was far too precious a dream.

Sunday, December 7, 1941, is a date deeply etched in the memories of millions of Americans. With the bombing of Pearl Harbor the United States was plunged into war. One day when Dad and I were working in the hatchery, he took time to tell a story which I had often heard through the years. But with my eighteenth birthday only a little over a year away, his account took on a new meaning.

Peaceful Holmes County, Ohio was far removed from two pistol shots fired in Austria on a June Sunday in 1914. But those shots echoed across Europe and ultimately around the world. Scarcely a month later Germany declared war on Russia, starting World War I, "the war to end all wars."

Three years later the first American troops set foot on French soil and soon encountered *Bluet and Isen* (blood and iron) which, according to Bismark's declaration in the eighteenth century, was the only way for great problems to be solved.

The United States passed a selective service law in May of 1917. Soon after the turn of the following year Dad turned twenty-one and received his personal greetings from President Wilson.

The Amish stem from the Anabaptists. These "rebaptizers" first flourished in Europe in the early 1500's as part of the Reformation. From the very first they were loyal to the civil government but refused to bear arms or take oaths.

The first recorded adult baptism was in 1525 in Zurich, the city of the great reformer, Zwingli. When many others soon followed, Protestants, Catholics, and secular governments determined to crush the new movement. Said Zwingli, "Let the man be drowned who baptizes a second time," and a veritable wave of persecution overwhelmed the hapless Anabaptists. During the next century and a half martyrdoms reached the appalling total of tens of thousands. These tortured lovers of peace finally fled to the seashores, and into the ships, and on to the New World. Many made their homes in Pennsylvania where William Penn offered them religious liberty.

The first Amish Mennonites came to the Quaker State in 1728. Jacob Hochstetler, my great, great, great, great, great, great grandfather, came to these shores a few years later.

Since Dad's religious life was composed mostly of obeying the strict rules of the Amish Church, he did not question the necessity of refusing to bear arms. He took his stand in spite of stories making the rounds in 1918 that by the time the army got through with Conscientious Objectors they were only too eager to shoulder a gun. The word was that some war-resisters were jailed, others beaten, and still others simply shot. Living in a community with very limited exposure to the outside world, Dad prepared for his army induction with dreadful surmisings.

The fateful day of parting came. Dad went to his room after the morning chores, hung his work pants on the bedpost, and donned his "Sunday clothes." When he said goodbye to his family and friends, crawled into the buggy with his father and mother, and headed out that long lane, it seemed like he was back in Europe with his persecuted forefathers again.

At the end of the lane they turned north for the short trip to Mount Hope, and then turned west on the long road to Millersburg and the train station. The horse jogged the eight miles slowly, and no one asked him to hurry.

They talked of their roots in Europe. The name, Hochstetler, meant "high settlement." This was not surprising for a people who originated among the Swiss Alps. (Dad and his brothers and sisters changed the name to Hostetler for convenience of spelling and pronunciation.)

They recounted their roots in this country. Dad's ancestor eight generations back was one of the earliest Amish settlers in Pennsylvania. Jacob Hochstetler bought a farm on the frontier (today Shartlesville, about fifty miles east of Harrisburg).

On a September night in 1757 the dog aroused the family with his persistent barking. Jacob Jr. opened the back door to investigate and saw shadowy forms behind the outdoor bake oven. A rifle cracked. Hit in his thigh, he staggered back and flung the door shut.

By this time Jacob and his two other teenage sons, Joseph and Christian, were peering out the windows. They saw eight or ten Indians standing near the bake oven. Secure in their log house, Joseph and Christian asked for permission to shoot the attackers. But Jacob Hochstetler held firmly to his peace convictions, and the price he paid was high.

The Indians set fire to the house and massacred his wife, Jacob Jr., and a young daughter. They then took Jacob and his two remaining sons captive, fleeing westward to Ohio.

Jacob escaped and returned home after three lonely years. Joseph and Christian, separated from their father and from each other, remained captive for two more years. Joseph all his days insisted that the family could have been saved if only his father had given consent to shoot since the men of the family were all excellent marksmen.

105

(Not long ago I visited the scene of the massacre. Another house now stands on the original foundation, and the bake oven has crumbled to the ground. I stood where the Indians must have stood those many years ago. The present owner gave me a stone from the oven. It rests on a shelf in our living room, along with other family treasures.)

As the buggy moved slowly on, Dad remembered the day in his early teens when he was bringing the cows from the pasture. He had looked up into the skies and prayed, "Oh God—if there is a God—arrange it so that somehow I will get to heaven." Later, when in his late teens, he was baptized and received into the church of his parents. Although he was faithful in attending the services, his unsatisfied longing for the assurance of eternal life was ever with him.

Arriving in Millersburg, Dad boarded the train and headed south to Camp Taylor in Kentucky. What a sight he must have been! Long hair, cut square at back and front, broadfall pants, cloth suspenders, hook and eye fasteners on his coat, black broad-brimmed hat, and button shoes. He was quaint and amusing—and scared.

Upon arrival at Camp Taylor he soon encountered a belligerent sergeant. When Dad revealed his position as a Conscientious Objector, the officer allowed that it wouldn't be long before he would have a change of mind. He said a few others had tried to be COs but had soon given in, so Dad was all alone.

Soon after being issued his army clothes, Dad was ordered to put them on. When he refused, he was castigated. And when that didn't produce the desired result, he was informed that COs who disobeyed orders were sometimes shot. He was then sent off to his quarters.

Some soldiers in the barracks derided the young Amishman when he walked in. Others treated him kindly. "That first night in camp," Dad would remember, "was the longest night of my life."

The next morning he was simply herded along with the rest to the mess hall for breakfast. When he happened to mention his fears of being shot to a barracks mate who seemed sympathetic, his friend was amazed and promptly reported the sergeant's threat to a superior officer. The officer immediately called the sergeant in and gave him a severe tongue-lashing. "Don't ever threaten anyone else that way," he ordered.

He then gave orders to have Dad join the other COs in the camp. The others? God be praised!

Dad walked over to another barracks where, to his great joy, he not only found fellow Conscientious Objectors but other Amishmen as well. They were soon jabbering away in their familiar Pennsylvania Dutch. The next day he joined them in the daily assignment of cleaning up the camp. The work was hard but the young farmers took it in stride.

When his peace position was challenged by soldiers who disagreed with him, Dad was embarrassed to discover that he did not really know what the Bible had to say on the subject. Actually, his only defense was that his church was against war. He was also questioned on other matters of doctrine and Amish tradition. Again, he was humiliated because he had no answers which satisfied either his questioners or himself.

For the first time in his life he began to study the Bible to see what it had to say. He soon discovered that he was a sinner with only one door of escape from eternal death. One night he knelt beside his army cot, confessed his sins, and accepted Jesus Christ as his savior.

What a wonderful assurance! What a blessed experience! Eli Hostetler was a new creation in the Lord. Dad said it was like walking on air.

As the summer of 1918 wore on, rumors were rampant that the war would soon end. Ironically, many soldiers in Camp Taylor became ill with the flu and measles. Because of limited medical know-how and the lack of modern drugs, more men died in the hospitals of Europe and the United States in the late stages of the conflict than perished on the battlefields.

Camp Taylor was no exception. Overworked doctors begged for more help to nurse the sick and the dying. When the COs passed the word along that they were willing to work as orderlies even among those with contagious diseases, their offer was quickly accepted. Some also became ill and a few joined the ranks of the dying. Although they were never given medals for their valor, both officers and enlisted men commended them for bravery in serving beyond the call of duty.

One night after the lights were dimmed, Dad heard a weak voice calling, "Water, someone *please* bring me water." The man was in another section of the hospital and under the care of an orderly who made no move to answer the plea.

Dad got a cup of cold water and walked over. When he came to the patient's bedside, he recognized him as the man who had been especially hateful to the COs. He was barely able to gulp the refreshing liquid, and later that night, as Dad put it, "Some men came in and carried him out."

Just a few days earlier Dad had come across the Bible verse which promised, "Whosoever shall give to drink unto one of these little ones a cup of cold water . . . , he shall in no wise lose his reward." As he thought about the promise, he felt an overpowering sense of the presence of God.

With the cool breezes of fall, the rumors of World War I being nearly over became more persistent. Suddenly, it came to an end. Armistice Day, November 11, 1918!

But the soldiers at Camp Taylor were still getting sick, and the sick were still dying. Dad and the other COs were retained to help in the hospitals even though many soldiers were being discharged. For the first time since being drafted, Dad was really homesick. How he longed for the hills of Holmes County.

His papers of honorable discharge were issued on a December day! His heart beat with excitement as the train wheels merrily clicked their way back to Millersburg. He had been gone less than a year, but measured in experience, it was much longer. He had gone away in uncertainty and fear. He returned with maturity and faith.

When young Eli arrived at home and walked into his own room again, he found his work pants right where he had hung them on the bedpost. No one had touched them in his absence. He quickly changed clothes and hurried to the barn and fields with his father and brothers. That evening his mother and sisters outdid themselves with the "seven sweets and seven sours" of German tradition, plus a lot more. Eli was safely home and the family was celebrating with abandon.

It was a good story, and Dad told it well. I thought some long, long thoughts about the historic peace position so staunchly supported by my ancestors for eight generations in America, and many years before. I decided to make it nine generations.

Chapter 19

BUS WHEELS

Not long after the bombing of Pearl Harbor, Dad decided to buy the old grain elevator in North Lawrence. He then sold the place on the hill which holds so many wonderful memories, and at which our family had lived for the remarkable total of eight years. In Mother's own words, "Up on the hill we stayed put the longest."

He bought a house in North Lawrence which was, and continues to be, the most beautiful house in town. The whole family loved that home. It set well back from the street in a spacious, tree-shaded lawn. The driveway wound majestically around the house. All of us thought we had finally "arrived," and hoped that no more moves were in our future.

In the fall of 1942 Dad and Mother put me on a bus and sent me off to Messiah College, near Harrisburg, Pennsylvania. Even though it was only 300 miles away, it represented a separation which, except for some summers at home, was permanent. In the succeeding years, all eight children went to Messiah College.

How Dad and Mother managed to do this from both a philosophical and financial standpoint, is beyond any reasonable explanation. Their own formal education was cut off about half way through grade school. What is more, their background called for children to work for their parents until they were twenty-one, turning over all earnings until then. At the very time they could have started to store up earthly treasures, they steadfastly turned their backs on such for the sake of their children.

Most of us registered at the college with a lot more faith than money. I stood in the registration line that first year at Messiah, knowing very well I didn't have nearly enough money to pay the first semester bill even with tuition less than $100. I finally stood before the business manager.

His name was Jesse Brechbill, and, as I learned later, he was an astute man of finances. With many tremblings I revealed my financial plight to him. He smiled and said there was a way. He would prepare a note and Dad would need to sign it. I bless the memory of that wonderful man who handled the whole matter with exquisite skill and kindness. I remember my pride in a father who was known even in far away Pennsylvania as one who paid his bills. In those moments I was transformed from the fear of rejection to the confidence of stature because my father had integrity.

One after the other, Dad signed notes for all his children. Sometimes we were able to pay them off ourselves. Sometimes Dad needed to. Somehow they always got paid by means of sweat and prayers.

After I went away to school, Eli Jr. became restless and rebellious. One evening he went to a movie in Massillon, eight miles away. In Dad's eyes, theatres were dens of iniquity, and strictly off-limits. When he learned that Junior had gone to watch the "ungodly Hollywood actors," he got into the car and headed for Massillon, late at night.

Eli Jr. was coming back home by way of a rather unsuccessful thumb when Dad came upon him by the wayside. Junior quietly crawled into the car and Dad simply brought him home, never saying a word. He seemed to know how to handle teenagers.

Later that year Eli Jr., rebellious as ever, decided he wanted to attend a Christian high school in Upland, California. Dad had a serious struggle with the problem, but in the end decided to allow his prodigal son to go although other members of the family, including myself, were opposed.

But Dad, as usual, had made the right decision after much prayer. Eli Jr. encountered a group of Godly teachers who got him straightened out in spite of himself. Upland College, where he attended, has since merged with Messiah College, but the good works of its California days are perpetuated in the lives of its appreciative graduates.

A number of years later I was being graduated from Messiah College with an arts degree. My brother, George, was receiving a junior college diploma, and my brother, Albert, was completing his high school work at the same place. The circumstance was so unusual that the college president asked Dad to have the invocation prayer at the commencement.

I was both delighted and apprehensive. Delighted because Dad had never received such an honor, and apprehensive

110

because he would certainly mangle the King's English. But it was not to be. The day before graduation we got a phone call from Ohio. Mother was ill, and Dad was staying with her. It was a lonely commencement although good friends were all around. And it was the only one Dad and Mother ever missed for any of their children.

It was my privilege to be selected as one of the graduates giving a speech, and I planned to honor Dad and Mother in one part of the talk entitled, "I Am Debtor." When I came to that place, I paid tribute to my parents and the sacrificing parents of the other seniors. The audience, I noted, was deeply moved, but my heart was many miles away in Ohio, with a dad and mother who loved their children almost as much as they loved God.

Dad was sold on the virtues of Christian education. Almost too much. In the year before I first attended Messiah, Peter J. Wiebe, an educator in the Brethren in Christ Church, and who had been directly involved in the founding of a number of Christian schools, was visiting our home in Ohio. P.J., as his friends lovingly called him, was talking on his favorite topic, and before long he and Dad were giving serious attention to the possibility of starting a Christian school right there in Ohio.

Typical of Dad, he responded with enthusiasm, and Mr. Wiebe promised that he would talk with him again on the matter. After he left, our family cornered Dad and brought some pretty strong evidence to bear against the notion of his becoming the first president of the North Lawrence (or whatever) Bible School.

Perhaps we should have let him do it. The townspeople might have renamed their village Eliville, or Hostetlerburg.

Well, Dad didn't open a school, much to our relief. If the school had been started, a certain eight children would have become alumni. They were *not* interested because they wanted to get their education where they could sing in the college choirs.

I tried out for Male Chorus the first year at Messiah and made it, mostly because in those war years there was a desperate need for male voices. Many boyish dreams have a way of never coming true. That one did.

The next summer, 1943, Dad was interested in having the Sippo Congregation sponsor a tent revival meeting with the

111

lively preacher from Pennsylvania, John Rosenberry, as the evangelist. Because some rather unsettling stories drifted westward across the mountains about this young firebrand, more cautious people at Sippo caused the vote to go against the proposal.

But Dad was not to be denied. After much prayer, he was convinced that the meeting was in God's will. So he asked the church leadership if they objected to his sponsoring the meeting himself, being fully responsible for the finances. They reluctantly agreed.

To the dismay, I am sure, of our neighbors in North Lawrence, the large tent was pitched on the large lawn beside our home. John Rosenberry arrived and the meetings began. John, to put it mildly, was different. He was funny, loud, direct, unpredictable, biblical, effective. He was God's man for the tent meeting that summer.

The singing was lively and loud. One quiet evening Ira Buchwalter heard music as he sat on his veranda two miles away. "Mother," he called, "come quick; angels are singing!" If the music carried to his home, imagine what it must have sounded like to the neighbors!

People came from far and near, and scores were converted. Many prayed through to a deeper commitment. The proper term to describe the experience then was "saved and sanctified." Numerous young people of the Sippo Church and neighboring fellowships "prayed through."

After the three-week meeting was history, Dad suggested that the young people start a prayer meeting of their own in addition to the regular one on Thursday nights. Thus the Young People's Prayer Meeting was born. The fired-up teenagers got on their knees and stayed there until everyone had prayed. Knees got sore but hearts were enlarged in the Holy Spirit.

In the spring of 1945 the Young People's Prayer Meeting group agreed that "it seemed good to the Holy Spirit and us" to sponsor a tent meeting of their own. The decision was reached to make the venture in a field near the village of East Greenville. Some people at Sippo tried to hold us back, but Dad urged us on.

One night at the regular youth prayer meeting we faced the question of who should preach for the tent services. In the two years since the John Rosenberry meeting, four of our group had expressed a call to the ministry: Robert Wengerd, my brothers Lloyd and Eli Jr., and myself. The group felt one of us should be the evangelist.

After praying fervently, someone suggested the biblical method of casting lots. Agreed. The discussion then centered on how many names should be used and in what way. The decision was Spirit directed and therefore wise. Six slips of paper were used. The four names were placed on four of them, the fifth piece simply said "all four," and the sixth one was left blank.

All of this was done with no adult heads present. I marvel in the memory!

The pieces of paper were folded and placed in a hat. Once again we knelt for prayer. God was near as our hearts were melted together. When we got up, one of our group picked up the hat, held it high, and shook it vigorously. Then he lowered it just enough to allow another prayer-partner to reach in.

The hand came away with the piece of paper. My thoughts raced. Would I be the preacher? Would one of the other three? Might all of us be in the lot? Would God perhaps say a definite No to each one?

The creases in the paper were carefully straightened out. The reader paused, and then choked out, "All four!" The moment was heavenly. The group was delighted. And we four neophyte preachers were both relieved and scared. We hadn't been rejected of God for that series, but now we had a job ahead of us.

As the older people of the church stood aside in admiration, the "young horses" pulled the load. It was a good meeting. Not as exciting as a John Rosenberry meeting, but a good meeting. The adults came to give their Amens and their dollars, making it possible for us to close the venture with all bills paid.

That fall various ones went off to college and other pursuits, but the group continued for a few more years. From that fellowship of youth came six ordained ministers who have preached in pastorates and missions in many parts of the United States and Canada. Four of the young women married ministers. Almost all of the two dozen or more people in the prayer group developed into strong church leaders and supporters.

113

Chapter 20

ROLLING WHEELS

The success of the North Lawrence tent meeting, combined with the spiritual growth of the young people converted in the series, made Dad ever more eager to get started in a mission work of his own. Much to the dismay of the whole family, he put up the beautiful North Lawrence house for sale. And what is worse, it sold almost at once.

Mother remembers, "I had to cry a little when our home sold so quickly, but I did not stand in Eli's way."

We temporarily moved into a building in town which had been used as a saloon. What an indignity! From the best house in town to the worst.

Dad started looking around in Massillon, a city of about 30,000, eight miles east of North Lawrence. Before long he found an apartment building on Ohio Avenue which "could easily be converted into a church." He went to work with his hands, making both pews and pulpit furniture.

Dad being Dad, he neither asked for nor received any kind of support from the Sippo Church nor the Brethren in Christ Church at large. Having finally settled on house construction as the chief means of his support, he happily pounded nails on week days, and exuberantly pounded the pulpit on Sundays.

The congregation at the Ohio Avenue location remained small. Dad soon felt the moving itch again and bought a storefront property at Hecks Corners, not far away. Again there was an awful amount of sawing and hammering to get it into shape. The work of the Lord opened there near the end of 1945 and prospered modestly. In 1947 the denominational Home Mission Board recognized Dad's project and legitimized it by taking it under its wing.

In that year Dad began his annual reports which were printed in the yearly *Handbook of Missions*. The very first report reads: "CHRISTIAN FELLOWSHIP MISSION, Massillon, Ohio, Eli and Lydia Hostetler, and Doris Rohrer."

114

(Doris, an old friend of the family, was the first of a fine succession of "mission workers" laboring in the Massillon harvest with Dad and Mother.)

He begins the report: "Behold, the Lord's hand is not shortened that it cannot save; neither His ear heavy that it cannot hear. Isa. 59:1." He then reports on the rally day crowd (165) and the quarterly revival meetings. Dad always had at least four revival meetings a year. His whole program orbited around these special times.

During such meetings Dad spent much time in prayer in addition to his regular morning and evening prayers. He even prayed for the evangelistic meetings when asking God's blessing on the food at mealtime. After one series of meetings was ended, he was praying at the table the next day. ". . . and help us to have a great victory over the devil in our meeting tonight," he fervently petitioned.

Realizing his mistake, he injected "O no, Lord, the revival's over." He then stammered to a rather unsuccessful conclusion as the rest of the family tried to keep pious faces!

In that same report Dad announced the purchase of "a large church which we are occupying since the first of July. We feel that the Lord has opened to us a large field since we have moved out of the little mission. Our new location is just one block from the railroad station. It was formerly a Baptist church."

He concludes the first report by saying, "Stop in and pay us a visit when you pass through Massillon. It will be very much appreciated."

In the years following many people accepted that invitation because the Lincoln Highway, U.S. Route 30, ran through the center of town, and also because Dad and Mother were great lovers of people.

"Just one block from the railroad station." It was handy for people catching trains, but the main line of the Pennsylvania Railroad reverberated with huge steam locomotives which showered soot all around in abundance. No wonder the Baptists agreed that Dad's mission was predestined to operate there!

In 1948 he reports a July revival meeting at which "seventy-six knelt at the altar for soul help and most of them got real victory." How Dad loved to have The Victory himself and to help others get the same.

115

Then came the radio ministry. "The last Sunday of November the mission staff started a half hour broadcast every Sunday over WAND, Canton, Ohio, 900 on the dial. This has opened to us a large field of labor. Many requests have come for prayer. We sometimes drive over fifty miles to pray for the sick. The Lord showed me over twenty years ago that some day I would preach the Gospel over the radio, and now I have the privilege."

He then goes on to reminisce. "It is 22 years since Sister Hostetler and I have been saved and sanctified. We can see God's hand on our lives through the years; we would have gone astray had it not been for Him. We say, 'Glory to God for His goodness to us.' It is just three years since we started mission work here in Massillon.

"We went through many trying experiences, especially the first year. One evening in prayer meeting I said I would not want to go through it again, but the Lord checked me the next morning in prayer and asked if I would not do it again for Him. I said, 'Yes, Lord, for You I would do it again.' These experiences have not affected our consecration, only deepened it. Praise our God forever!"

Dad was a very emotional person and a somewhat unregulated preacher when it came to ending his messages. He could get away with this in church services, but a 29-minute radio program was another matter. More than once he was still going strong when the program manager had to cut him off.

In the opening years of the radio ministry my two sisters, Lois and Evangeline, and Doris Rohrer provided trio music for the broadcast. The Sunshine Trio worked out a system which helped Dad get stopped in time. Using a song which was exactly three minutes long, they would begin singing softly at another microphone three minutes before the program had to end. With this amount of warning, Dad could unwind and get into his closing prayer. Even then, he often had only seconds to spare! When Dad got his boiler fired up for preaching, the pressure stayed up for a long time.

The outreach of the radio ministry was wide. Many stories could be related of conversions and healings. Here is an example. One night when Dad and Mother were attending a revival meeting at a Nazarene Church, a lady stood to give her testimony of her conversion.

Pointing to Dad she said, "I'm sure you don't know it, but during one of your Sunday broadcasts I was on top of our kitchen table hanging wall paper. I listened to your sermon, and near the end you said, 'Wherever you are, come and put your hand on your radio while I pray for you.' So I climbed down off the table, laid my hand on the radio, and God saved me."

My Dad cried and shouted that evening.

His ministry was fruitful in other ways. In 1949 he reported: "We are happy to have been able to send out two young couples in the past year into active mission work. Brother and Sister Robert Wengerd went to the Kentucky field, and Brother and Sister Eli Hostetler, Jr. have taken up their work in the Life Line Gospel Mission in San Francisco."

In 1950 a total of 173 seekers were reported and more than 200 anointed for healing, many of the latter in response to the radio ministry. "We know of two divorce suits which have been dropped and the families restored."

The next year's report mentions an unusual watchnight service on New Year's Eve. "We gathered around the altar for prayer till about 4:00 a.m. A young man . . . prayed through just before the meeting broke up. Someone suggested we are starting out the New Year in high gear. Another brother said, 'Let's get it into overdrive.' Everybody said, 'Amen!' "

Dad began his 1952 report with a favorite scripture verse: "He that goeth forth and weepeth, bearing precious seed, shall doubtless come again with rejoicing, bringing his sheaves with him," and reports a successful year.

In this report he first mentions new outposts. "Due to our radio work, many of these seekers (in the evangelistic meetings) are from . . . quite a distance. All the additions to the church are from the Uniontown and Shanesville areas." Very shortly after this, Dad organized separate congregations at both places. The Shanesville work to the south produced a fine young preacher (out of the Amish Church) who subsequently pastored the Massillon Church after serving in Kentucky. The Uniontown fellowship, north of Massillon, built a fine new church.

Because of his increasing church activities, Dad's construction projects slowed down. When an ad appeared in the Massillon paper with an opening for a service station operator, he decided to venture in the gas-pumping business even though the location was poor and three successive previous operators had gone broke.

The venture was short-lived. Wages for needed help plus lease costs outstripped income from the first.

But Dad, ever the optimist, took off in another business direction which was intended to provide income while freeing him for more church ministries. He bought a few apartment buildings and went through the throes of dealing with renters who always seemed to be out of money, out of sorts, or out of town.

The main problem, however, was that the heavy mortgages ate up the profits. The whole worrisome situation, extending over a number of years, never became financially successful. When the apartments were finally sold, Dad barely received enough clear cash to pay off the loans.

In 1953 the report tells of a joint business meeting for the three congregations at which the decision was reached for the Uniontown people to have their own council the following year. "All members of council felt encouraged to press forward and be more evangelistic for the coming year."

The next year Dad reports that the work at Massillon "is largely among the poor people. Sometimes a drunkard comes into the service. One who came and made fun remained to pray at the altar. Another drunkard was graciously saved and his home has been transformed. The entire family are now coming to church."

The reports of victory in the camp continued in 1955. In 1956 the Handbook of Missions had separate reports from Massillon and the two outposts. In 1957 the Massillon Mission was changed to a Mission Pastorate, an intermediate step to becoming a full-fledged congregation. That was the last year for Dad and Mother in Massillon; they moved to Sarasota, Florida soon after and others took up their mantle.

When their successors, Rev. and Mrs. Glen Ressler, reported in 1958 they said, "The former pastor, Rev. Eli Hostetler, Sr., and wife continued the work until September. They served faithfully and well, and were granted a leave of absence as they desired."

That marked the end of the Massillon ministry for them, a total of thirteen years, by far the longest time Dad and Mother lived in one place. Once again the urge to move on caused them to leave friends and home.

The Massillon congregation has since relocated and built a beautiful new church on the edge of town, far away from the dirt and noise of trains and traffic. The downtown church has been demoted to a parking lot.

Chapter 21

LOVE'S WHEELS

Dad and Mother "retired" to Florida soon after completing their work in Massillon, buying a small property in Sarasota. Dad was sixty years old but a long way from being worn out either physically, emotionally, or spiritually. Our family was scattered in many places: Ontario, New York, Kentucky, Pennsylvania, Michigan, California, and Ohio.

It wasn't long until Dad and Mother began writing about having a prayer meeting group. Word soon came that the group had agreed to purchase a building in Fruitville, just outside Sarasota. Once again Dad went happily to work with hammer and saw, converting some rooms into a sanctuary and making beautiful mahogany pews and pulpit furniture.

And once again he did all of this without checking in with the denominational church leaders. This was the fourth congregation he helped get started. I suppose if he had waited for all the proper administrative moves, the family home would still be in North Lawrence, Ohio!

Bishop Henry Ginder was the overseer of the regional conference which included Florida. One day in 1958 he received a phone call from Dad, and the conversation went something like this.

Dad: "Hello, Bishop Ginder, I called to tell you that we have a Brethren in Christ congregation in Fruitville."

(Bishop Ginder was surprised. In all of his administrative experience, he had always been involved with the beginnings of new congregations. But he, as is the custom with wise bishops, played it cool.)

Bishop: "I am very glad to hear the good news, Eli. Have you already received members into your church?"

Dad: "No, Bishop, we didn't although we almost went ahead. Actually, that is my reason for calling. I would like for you to come as soon as possible and conduct a reception service for charter members."

(Bishop Ginder was somewhat relieved; things seemed to be a bit more under control.)

Bishop: "I will be very happy to come as soon as I can arrange it. Where are you holding your services?"

Dad: "Oh, I forgot to tell you. We found a good building for a church, and I have been remodeling it. We have some tithers around here, and a good part of the building is already paid for!"

Bishop: "The Lord is really blessing you people! Have you had a dedication service for your church?"

Dad: "No, but I'd like you to arrange one."

(Bishop Ginder didn't wait long to make his first visit. He didn't dare! When he arrived on a Saturday, a congregational council was held with elections conducted for a deacon, a treasurer, and a church board. None of these were members of the church until the next day when the church was also dedicated. Bishops sometimes need to do unconventional things when pushed by impetuosity! The next denominational directory listed the Fruitville Church.

Dad and Mother really enjoyed the Florida sunshine. When the weather was pleasant in the wintertime and their local media emphasized the frigid temperatures in the North, they always mentioned the weather in their letters. But when the frost line dipped into the Sunshine State, nary a word was said about the weather.

They appreciated the warmth and citrus and fishing so much that they launched a plan to bring all their children to Florida for a visit—with Dad and Mother footing the bill. The first winter of the plan, 1958, our family and my sister Vange's family were invited. But there were conditions.

Dad and Mother considered the necktie an unnecessary evil, an obvious device to show off pride. So our invitation came with the stipulation that all neckties be left in snow country. That wouldn't have been all that difficult for me except that Dad insisted I preach in his church while in Florida.

When Uncle Sam, who was more efficient in those days, speeded my missive to Florida, it carried the information that our family very much wanted to come to Florida but that we could not come on the prescribed terms. We then sat back and waited for fatherly love to respond.

To our distress the reply expressed regret. "Sorry you are not coming," was the essence of the message. He informed us that they would ask another member of the family. I guess I should have known better than call Dad's bluff (which really wasn't a bluff at all) in the first place. I quickly abandoned Uncle Sam and grabbed the nearest Alexander Graham Bell.

Dad came on the line, friendly as ever. "Look Dad, we have reconsidered your invitation and will plan to come after all. Is that O.K. with you?"

"Sure, Paul," he responded, "just be sure to shut your back door when you come so all that cold weather stays up north!" He didn't say anything about the offending neckwear. Dad didn't believe in hitting a fellow when he was down.

We drove to Florida from near Buffalo, New York. By the second day we put our coats into the car trunk to stay. We had a wonderful time in many ways, including fishing. Many fish were pulled in from the bridges which spanned the tidal waters in the harbor. But one whole day was set aside for deep sea fishing.

Dad hauled us all out of bed at an unearthly hour so that we could be the first persons in line on the dock for the boat which held fifty fishermen. He insisted that one could always catch more fish from the back of the boat. We did a lot of grumbling about the outrageous hour, but complied in order to humor Dad. How on earth (or in the sea) could the fish know which end of the boat we were fishing from?

When the gate to the gangplank opened, our crowd of six hurried to the fantail of the boat and staked out our positions. It happened that the boat was just six places wide at the stern. The other forty-four people lined the rail around the rest of the boat, and we were soon on our way.

When we arrived where the fishing was supposed to happen, a crew member came around asking for fifty cents per head for the biggest-fish pool. I quickly multiplied fifty times fifty and came up with $25. Not bad. But Dad looked the man sternly in the eye and informed him our group was not interested.

Dad barely had his line in the water until he had action, soon landing a fish. The rest of us began jerking and reeling away also. We were busy pulling on our lines all day long. Our catch included octopuses, small sharks, and poisonous eels. We hauled aboard trigger fish, flounders, and amber jacks, but we much preferred our good take of red and black groupers.

When the amber jacks struck, always in large schools,

things got exciting in a hurry. These fish, usually about two feet long, would charge around much like a lake bass, causing lines to become entangled.

One overly-enthusiastic amber jack managed to cross over under the hull and whipped around a line on the other side. In a moment, two men were shouting that they had hooked onto the biggest catch of the day. They heaved away with all their might until one of the crew obligingly pointed out that if they didn't stop "they would lift the boat right out of the water!"

Our group of six not only caught more fish per person than anyone else, we caught *many* more. Some people within ten feet of us never caught a fish all day! At one location, people at the front of the boat complained to the captain about our continuing good luck, and he said, "I'll fix that." He weighed the anchor, allowing the boat to drift back. We continued to catch fish and the fishermen at the far end continued to experience frustration.

Dad's insistence that we get out of bed early paid off, even though he had no reasonable explanation. "Only the fish know why," smiled Dad. Who could argue with that?

When all lines were pulled in for the trip back to shore, a crew member came around to find the biggest fish for the pool payoff. Dad was declared the winner! but he did not receive the prize because he had not entered the pool. He had paid $5 each for his five guests on the boat. When he told him the Lord wanted to reward his generosity, he frowned, but his eyes twinkled.

When Sunday came we all went to Dad's new church. It was very small but showed evidence of Dad's loving craftmanship. As a fisherman, Dad knew how to pull them in with enthusiasm and skill. But as a fisher-of-men, he was much more devoted and skillful. As I sat there in church (Dad always went early) and looked out the open windows at the heavily laden orange groves, I thanked God for my father and mother.

My hand caressed the beautiful pew Dad had fashioned with his own hands, and I thought of his love for the Brethren in Christ Church and his faithful attendance of the General Conferences. He had many friends at those annual convocations of the brotherhood, but Dad never rose in the ranks. His highest achievement at the denominational level was serving as a member of the St. Petersburg Camp Board.

I remembered my first trip to General Conference as a nine year old. The choice happening of that trip to Ludlow Falls, Ohio, was Dad's purchase of a large and colorful Egermeier's Bible story book. It was expensive, but Dad said he couldn't afford not to have it.

I read that book from cover to cover many times. I savored its stories and pondered its pictures. It gave me a better Bible background and understanding than did much more scholarly volumes in later years.

My recollections jumped to the next year (1935) when Dad and Mother took their three oldest sons to General Conference north of Toronto, Ontario, Canada. When we stopped for a picnic lunch by the roadside, everyone was so interested and hungry that an important item was overlooked. Dad sat down and discovered too late that the leg under his corner of the picnic table was missing.

His two hundred pounds quickly tipped the table toward him although we boys were already seated on the opposite side! Everything on the table slid in his direction, including the milk jug. His look of consternation was priceless. We didn't know if we dared laugh, but we did anyhow.

Dad got up and brushed the food off his clothes while Mother used water to wash off the milk. "For pity sakes," complained Dad, "what a way for a delegate to General Conference to get treated!"

I thought about the 1939 General Conference on the campus of Messiah College. Our family was quartered in a tent. A nearby tent housed another preacher and his wife. Early one morning he was talking to her. Tent walls are thin, and every word was clearly audible to Dad.

The preacher told his wife with some pride that someone had told him he remembered a sermon he had preached forty years before. After a pause to let that profound statement sink in, he declared, "That is *powerful* preaching!" Dad chuckled until he realized that even that slight sound might carry to the next tent.

In the years that followed, the story became a family joke. When anyone remarked that he remembered what Dad had said in a sermon, we would look at Dad in mock seriousness and say, "*That* is *powerful* preaching!" It helped keep him humble.

The brotherhood and the Conference were very important to Dad. One year while he was still tilling the small muck farm, contrary weather made it impossible for area farmers to plant their corn at the usual time. Their aim was always to have corn at least "knee-high by the 4th of July."

The rains finally stopped and allowed farmers to plant their corn in early June, just when it was time for Dad to spend a week at General Conference. To some farmers, this did not pose a problem—they planted their corn. But for Dad it was a struggle. General Conference won out, and when the 4th of July rolled around his corn was knee-high to Tom Thumb.

Now, I wish it could be reported that the Lord rewarded Dad for his devotion to the church. But not so. An early frost caught the corn before it was ready to harvest and the grain shrivelled on the cob.

Good Christian farmers on adjoining farms were amused with the second-rate farmer and his crops. What they didn't comprehend was that Dad was growing children first, and then corn, while they had it the other way. Years later their bank accounts brought them small comfort as they suffered through the heartbreak of straying children.

All these thoughts and many more passed through my mind before the service began.

Dad opened the service in his typical way. Looking us all over carefully, he asked, "Everyone happy?" He smiled his big, loving smile. "Too many Christians look like they ate a sour pickle or lost their last friend. All of us have much to be happy about, blessed be the name of Jesus!"

By the time we began the opening song, even the chronic non-smilers looked more cheerful.

I preached the morning message, with Dad, as always, leaning forward in his seat and Amening me on.

A few days later we travelled back to the chilly North, laden with oranges, tangerines, and grapefruit. Our skins were darkened by the Florida sunshine, and our hearts brightened by father and mother love.

Chapter 22

GLORY WHEELS

Dad became interested in mission work among the Cuban refugees in Miami in the early 60's. He and Mother made the long, 200-mile trek from Sarasota many, many times, packing their station wagon full of clothes which they gathered in all possible ways.

One day Dad learned that some Cubans were reluctant to be identified with him because from their viewpoint his beard identified him with Fidel Castro. Dad was beyond his mid-sixties, and the beard was very much a conscience and habit part of him, but he put the razor to it.

That was Dad. He still held unyieldingly to certain matters of conscience relating to outward appearance, but he banished his beard when it interferred with his spiritual ministry to needy people.

In 1965 the Fruitville Congregation decided to build a wing on their church, accepting Dad's offer to do most of the work. And so once again he cheerfully sawed and pounded. And every week or so he pounded the miles to Miami to help with the Cuban mission work.

I was pastoring in Toronto at the time. The telephone rang on the Saturday before Easter. My brother Eli Jr. told me Mother had called from Florida, and that Dad had been taken to the hospital. No further word came to us on Easter.

Our phone rang once again on Monday morning. I was sitting in the church study along with Bishop Henry Ginder who had preached for our Holy Week services. The few words of that telephone message cut me to the heart. "Dad died this morning. He failed to recover from a massive cerebral hemorrhage."

I replaced the receiver mechanically and sat there in shock. I looked across the desk to Bishop Ginder. "Dad's gone." He came around the desk to comfort me and then prayed.

We went to the parsonage to tell my wife. As we went, I remarked, "You know, I suddenly feel ten years older."

Two of the children immediately went to Mother's side. A few days later we made our sorrowful pilgrimage to Massillon, Ohio. The earthly part of Dad had been brought to a funeral home there. I walked into the stillness and found Dad resting among the banks of flowers. It was the first time I saw him without a beard.

He looked healthy, but dark. Had the Florida funeral director failed to do his work properly, I wondered? And then I realized that Dad simply had a rich Florida tan. Stricken in the midst of pastoring and carpentering, he went home to Glory in his 69th year.

As I stood there, a whole flood of memories washed down over my soul. Joys. Sorrows. Regrets.

Dad was a non-conformist, and his ways had often embarrassed me. His clothes were always neat and clean, but he never felt the need to have his trousers pressed. As a result, when he stood at attention, his pants stood at ease. He always removed the buttons from the sleeves of his suit jackets "because they don't serve any purpose."

I remembered how, as a boy, I was ashamed of him because he was the only man in our community who wore a beard. When going to the city with Dad and Mother, I either raced ahead on the sidewalk or lingered far behind, to their exasperation. I never told them why. Now the beard was gone, and I missed it.

Ah, the follies of childhood and youth. If one could only go back and undo them.

Fortunately, things have a way of evening out. Although my pants manage to stand at attention along with me, my daughters are frequently scandalized by the color combinations I wear. When they complain, I sometimes change my tie or shirt. But at other times I stand steadfast. Dad would be pleased.

I thought of his active prayer life and the many times he fasted. He would get up early in the morning and pray long and loud. House guests always heard him, and more than one mentioned his prayer vigils with deep gratitude, saying that Dad always included them in his petitions.

He also prayed for each of his children, their spouses, and the grandchildren by name. He often declared "that the devil will not get any of my children unless he does so over my dead body."

When the windows were open, the neighbors also heard his hearty praises and tearful pleas. As he grew older, his prayers became longer. Mother taped his prayer one morning in the last year of his life. Each member of the family treasures a copy.

While I meditated on these things beside his casket, a completely new thought struck me.

My father, who had bounced around from pillar to post as a jack of all trades through the years, was a man of achievement. While countless other preachers had been going about their work in a much more organized and acceptable way, Dad had quietly started a dozen prayer meeting groups and founded four congregations.

And all the while, he was a man who "ruled his own household well." His three oldest sons were ministers, both daughters were married to clergymen, and the three youngest sons were high school teachers. All, like Dad, delighted in making things with their hands. And all, like Dad and Mother, loved the church and were active in it.

Up to that moment I had been convinced from my teen years that I would make a greater impact in my corner of the world than Dad had on his. But now I saw it would never happen. It was humbling.

That evening friends and relatives poured into the funeral home from far and near. Many told of how his good life had helped them and how they remembered his sermons of years before. "That *was* powerful preaching," I mused.

The next day the funeral service was held in the Sippo Church, and thus Dad came home to his beginnings of thirty-five years before.

The little church was packed. The service was one of victory and rejoicing. In response to the urging of friends, Dad's six sons stood beside the casket and sang, "I Want My Life to Tell for Jesus." We chose the song because he liked it so much and also because we felt it outlined Dad's way of life.

> Amid life's busy, hurried throng,
>   The gay, the sad, the weak, the strong—
> While I am travelling along,
>   I want my life to tell for Jesus.
>
> I want to be a beacon light
>   To show wayfarers in the night,

And lead them in the way aright,
    I want my life to tell for Jesus.

To wealth and fame I would not climb,
    But I would know God's peace sublime,
And everywhere and all the time,
    I want my life to tell for Jesus.

Following the service we travelled slowly through the familiar countryside to the Pleasant View Cemetery where we soberly returned "dust to dust."

All his life Dad was a preacher on wheels, moving again and again in his quest for the better life. In the move from his earthly tabernacle he found it.